Battered Black Women and Welfare Reform

*Between a Rock
and a Hard Place*

Dána-Ain Davis

STATE UNIVERSITY OF NEW YORK PRESS

Published by
State University of New York Press, Albany

For information, address State University of New York Press,
194 Washington Avenue, Suite 305, Albany, NY 12210-2384

Cover photo of the Brick Wall, Savannah, Georgia, courtesy of Deirdre Davis.

Production by Diane Ganeles
Marketing by Anne M. Valentine

Library of Congress Cataloging in Publication Data

Davis, Dána-Ain, 1958-
  Battered Black women and welfare reform : between a rock and a hard
place / Dána-Ain Davis.
       p. cm. — (SUNY series in African American studies)
  Includes bibliographical references and index.
  ISBN-13: 978-0-7914-6843-2 (hardcover : alk. paper)
  ISBN-10: 0-7914-6843-7 (hardcover : alk. paper)
  ISBN-13: 978-0-7914-6844-9 (pbk. : alk. paper)
  ISBN-10: 0-7914-6844-5 (pbk. : alk. paper)
  1. Abused women—United States. 2. Welfare recipients—United States.
  3. African American women—United States. 4. Public welfare—United
States. I. Title. II. Series.

HV1445.D38 2006
362.5'5680820973—dc22

2005025792

10 9 8 7 6 5 4 3 2 1

I dedicate this book to the memory of my grandmother,
Angie Ashley Hall,
and all my relations.

Contents

vii

Foreword

August 2005 marks the ninth anniversary of Congressional passage of the Personal Responsibility and Work Opportunity Reconciliation Act (PRWORA), popularly known as "welfare reform." Despite repeated claims by key policymakers that welfare restructuring (the term "reform" is a misnomer) is a success and should be celebrated as such, Dána-Ain Davis joins other researchers whose rigorous research challenges this claim.

Battered Black Women and Welfare Reform is a powerful book that deserves to be read widely. The book should, if read with open minds and hearts by those who make and implement welfare policy, compel changes in national and state welfare policies. For anyone who imagines that welfare policy promotes improved economic well-being and security, opportunity, self-sufficiency, and hope for poor women and their families, this book is a wake-up call. But Davis goes further than many, documenting how racism infuses both the welfare policies that directly affect the Black women she worked with, and also the jobs they do and don't get, their relatively limited housing and child-care options, and, often, how they are viewed and treated by landlords, human service workers, potential employers, bosses, and many others.

For those of us not intimately involved with welfare restructuring, who are not members of families who live "reform," or welfare workers and administrators who implement welfare-to-work policies, or community advocates who assist families facing great hardship because of these policies, *Battered Black Women and Welfare Reform* takes us into the lives of 22 women who live at the nexus of poverty, violence, and the welfare system. Most of what counts as "knowledge" in this field comes either from large-scale studies that substitute statistics for human experience, satisfying a mind and heart-numbing confidence that that such knowledge is scientifically rigorous, or from thousands of anecdotes served up by reporters since 1996 to "humanize" newspaper, radio, or television stories about welfare. Dána-Ain Davis gives us something different. She takes us into the kind of community less often studied or reported on, far from the inner cities that have captured the attention of most scholars, to the kind of place where most of America's poor live. These are smaller cities and towns across the country with economies that have been dramatically affected by deindustrialization, divestment, and globalization. She takes us into the lives of women and children who have lived with violence and abuse, sometimes over the long haul, sometimes for shorter periods, but always with profound results. She focuses on Black women and their children, and through their experiences shows us that social service workers and landlords are neither colorblind nor always fair or humane. She shows us that racism is deeply intertwined with a host of public welfare policies, as well as with private practices. And she does all this with an unwavering commitment to tell the truth about women who themselves understand that their own lives belie the truth of racialized stereotypes about women on welfare, and who also know they are nevertheless judged and often treated as though they *were* the living embodiments of those stereotypes.

Davis begins her introduction with the reminder that "the clock is ticking," a reference to federal and state time limits on welfare receipt. These time limits essentially say to poor women and children: it does not matter whether there are jobs that are available and can support you, or if there is decent housing or child care you can afford, it does not matter that you have been subjected to violence and abuse or that you are trying to keep your children safe or to give them the kind of home that might help keep them from enduring what you have gone through. But Davis shows us that *it does matter.*

To stick with the image of the ticking clock, let me say to readers of this book, you are unlikely to lift your eyes to the clock while you are reading it. This is a beautifully written book that brings great insight, honesty, clarity, and humanity to a public policy debate that has marginalized and silenced women such as those whose stories fill these pages. But time will not stand still while you read this book. While the stories recounted in this book are in the past, other stories are being lived at this moment, stories of other Black women enduring the "ceremonies of degradation," the practices of regulation, the "theaters of maternal and child-care politics," the "strategic missions," and the "meticulous rituals of power and structural violence" that Davis elucidates in the following pages. As you read and afterwards, remember, the clock *is* ticking.

Sandra Morgen
University of Oregon, Eugene

Acknowledgments

This book would not have been possible without the courageous women, advocates, and community residents who shared their stories with me. I thank them for their time and energy.

Professors Shirley Lindenbaum, Leith Mullings, and Ida Susser were instrumental in guiding me through graduate school and the first draft of this book, which was my dissertation. Thank you for seeing me through it all.

Purchase College has been a blessing. I am very lucky to work with students who constantly astound and invigorate. Thank you for strengthening my commitment to teaching: Shantay Armstrong, Dion Bridges, Lindsay Charles, Noel Cole, Amber Galeo, Claire Henry, Acrea Mcintosh, Wali Muhammad, David Outerbridge, Rebecca Pelletier, Amanda Diva Seales, and Laura Zapata.

What would the academy be without amazing colleagues? Just some who offer constant support and direction are Zehra Arat, Karen Baird, Linda Bastone, Kim Christensen, Rudolf Gaudio, and Connie Lobur. I especially want to thank John Howard and Robert C. Smith who thought that this book should be published. I also want to thank Michael Rinella and Diane Ganeles for guiding this book to completion.

A special acknowledgement and debt of gratitude must go to Leith Mullings. Your humility, support, guidance, mentorship and friendship have profoundly influenced how I move in the world. Thank you for everything.

A close circle of ever inspiring sister/friends have held my hand and my heart: Deb Amory, Ana Aparicio, Christa Craven, Catlin Fullwood, Gail Garfield, Michelle Hay, Lorraine Herbst, Sue Hyatt, Michelle Johnson, Paula Johnson, Mamadi Matlhako, Andrea Queeley, Beth Richie, Andrea Williams, and Donna Wiltshire.

I also want to thank the fabulous women of Sister Scholars, an amazing group of activist-scholars whose laughter, love and keen intellectualism have filled me up over the last two and a half years. Thank you to Asale-Angel Ajani, Farah Jasmine Griffin, Kim Hall, Diane Harriford, Monica Miller, Mignon Moore, Jennifer Morgan, Leith Mullings, and Cheryl Mwaria. In addition, there are five other people whose intellectualism pushes me beyond whatever boundaries I may think exist: Greg Tate, Jeff Maskovsky, Sandra Morgen, John Clarke and Manning Marable.

Last but not least, I'd like to thank my family whose love is the foundation from which all things flow: Cynthia Wells, Ricci Scott, John and LaFredia Davis, Deirdre Davis and Dan Hanessian.

Aché

Introduction

The Clock is Ticking

When I arrived in a city I am calling Laneville, New York, in February 1998, the volume was rising about the implementation and restrictive nature of welfare reform. And, although battered women's advocates were challenging the implications of the policy, I was not focused on the issue. Without fully intending to, I shifted the focus of my anthropological research from examining the social processes of sheltering battered women to examining the interaction between welfare reform and Black battered women. Laneville is an interesting city in which to examine welfare reform policy, since it and the county in which it is located had undergone major economic changes. An area's economy, reflective of broader global processes, is an important factor in relation to how poor women might or might not achieve welfare reform's supposed goal of "self-sufficiency." In cities and towns across the United States, too few jobs are available, and race still influences opportunity. When the social problem of domestic violence intersects with these issues, the confluence of welfare reform, violence, race, and local economics becomes even more complicated. This ethnography examines the impact of welfare reform in terms of violence, race, and place. Specifically, it looks at what happens when poor Black battered women living in an economically compromised city try to create safe households while meeting welfare reform mandates.

1

By the time I left Laneville in 2000, the national press was falling all over itself with glowing accounts of welfare reform's success. Women were "working," the rolls were dropping, and the public was "free" at last from the burden of the unmotivated poor. But a competing story surfaced during my research, suggesting that for many women, the reality is otherwise. The simplistic representations in the press were repudiated by what the women I met went through to get assistance and what their lives were like after they received it.

I must admit that when President Clinton signed the Personal Responsibility and Work Opportunity Reconciliation Act (PRWORA, or The Act) of 1996, my attention was not fully directed toward national welfare policy debates or their implications for women and poor people of color, or the practices that would be used in its implementation. Then one year later, after the federal legislation passed and just a few months after Governor Pataki signed the Welfare Reform Act of New York in 1997, the first "Trapped by Poverty/Trapped by Abuse" conference was held in Chicago. The conference goal was to develop research agendas to expand projects linking domestic violence and welfare use, and to investigate the relationship between domestic violence and welfare policy. But few at the conference discussed race beyond using it as a descriptor. At that time I wondered how race would factor into women's chances of achieving economic self-sufficiency, but still I did not pursue this as a research question. Instead, I continued to focus on the processes of sheltering battered women. I selected my research site and spent the next twenty-two months at Angel House Shelter for battered women in the city of Laneville located in River Valley County, New York.

My inattention to welfare reform was short-lived. On March 27, 1998, just a few weeks after being in the field, I was asked to drop off paperwork at the River Valley County Department of Social Services (RVCDSS) for one of the women living at the shelter who was applying for assistance. I had never sat in a welfare office but had applied for social services at a community-based health organization in the 1980s and found that process and the paperwork demanding and confusing. As I sat in the RVCDSS waiting room, the first thing that caught my attention was a poster of a clock resting on an easel. The caption read, "The Clock is Ticking." The poster's message was part of a campaign to raise welfare recipients' awareness that welfare had changed. PRWORA shifted responsibility of providing assistance to poor and working-class people from the federal to the state level, a process known as devolution. The law replaced the old welfare program, Aid to Families with Dependent Children (AFDC) with a new program called Temporary Assistance to Needy Families (TANF), which now meant among other things, women or recipients would no longer be assured of government support for as long as they needed it. Rather they would only receive assistance for a maximum of five years over their lifetime. Furthermore, the law mandated that recipients would have to work in order to receive assistance. The Act's goals were influenced by conservative policy analysts and resolved tensions surrounding welfare use including the long-standing (and erroneous) belief that welfare recipients lacked morals and values. These positions were taken by right-wing scholars (see for example Mead 1986a) and others who argued that poor people were inappropriately dependent on government aid and that such aid fostered "a way of life" (Lewis 1966; Auletta 1982;Wilson 1984). Even President Clinton, argued that welfare reform would ". . . transform a broken system that traps too many people in a cycle of dependence to one that emphasizes work and independence . . ." (*New York Times* 8/1/96). Welfare reform, which achieved bipartisan support, would redirect idleness and foster "self-sufficiency" by making people work or be engaged in work-related activities in order to remain eligible for cash and other benefits. If the work obligation is not met, then people run the risk of being sanctioned. Sanctions come in the form of having benefits such as food stamps, transfer payments for housing, Medicaid, and/or cash benefits reduced or eliminated for a specified period of time or having cases closed.

Changes in welfare were of concern to advocates and researchers working with or on behalf of battered women. Having made connections between violence, poverty, and welfare at least since the early 1990s, many critiqued the mandatory work component of welfare reform. Several analyses were offered. First, women who are economically dependent upon their abusers have few means of support and public assistance provides an opportunity for them to leave abusive situations (Davis and Kraham 1995). Second, abusers often maintain control over their victims by inflicting physical and psychological injuries, preventing some women from complying with their state's work requirements. Third, time limitations for assistance might push families deeper into poverty. And, finally, the inability to comply with mandates means losing benefits and possibly staying or returning to abusers due to the need for economic support (Brandwein 1999; Kurz 1999).

Out of these critiques a protective measure for battered women was amended to the Federal PRWORA. It is known as the Family Violence Option (FVO [Sec. 402(a) (7)]. The FVO was sponsored by Senators Paul Wellstone (D-Minnesota) and Patti Murray (D-Washington) and permits states, if they chose to implement it, to screen welfare recipients for domestic violence, refer victims of domestic violence to counseling, and determine whether certain welfare requirements should be waived (Kurz 1999). The FVO was adopted by New York thanks to the efforts of battered women's advocates. Of course, the issue of domestic violence, poverty, and welfare utilization was and continues to be important, but in critiquing welfare reform, the particular impact of this measure on Black women who are battered women and have left their abusers has been missing from the discussion. Amplifying Black women's experience is important because, as has been argued elsewhere, negative images of them were used strategically in building public support for welfare reform encouraging erroneous associations between race and poverty specifically linking race and welfare (Neubuck and Cazenave 2001; Hancock 2004). A consuming public was fed a seemingly never-ending spectacle of Blacks on welfare nourishing the belief that welfare programs "benefit" Blacks (Gilens 1999; Domke, McCoy, and Torres 1999). Most often constructed as cheats and frauds, the media, politicians, and scholars, strengthen the negative discourse that circulates around Black women and welfare. Of course any discussion of discourse may lead us to focus only on representations of disempowerment rather than actual lack of power and the implications therein. But the circulation of this discourse must certainly be linked to material circumstances. Thus, this ethnography examines the material impact of welfare reform by evaluating critical aspects of welfare reform policy, from the social service caseworker/client interaction to the role played by economic shifts and preexisting structures of racial inequality in constructing women's life chances. Because race bears on the fates of women subjected to welfare reform, as you read this ethnography, you will see how Black women "lived" welfare policy in the space where intimate violence, race, changes in the composition of employment brought about by deindustrialization, and gentrification, intersect. It illustrates the many ways in which welfare reform policy is a form of structural violence; that is, the ways in which possibilities for survival are regulated and disrupted by policy.

Methodology

After visiting battered women's shelters in four counties in New York State, I chose the city of Laneville located in River Valley County, New York, as the research site for several reasons. First, the county had implemented welfare reform policy in August 1997, six months before my research began, and I was able to examine the initial effects of the new law. Second, Laneville is a small city, and unlike large multicity studies of urban areas such as Chicago, Los Angeles, and Harlem (see for example Quint, Edin, et al. 1999; Newman 1999), it is a geographic area rarely explored in the literature on welfare. One way in which this project is unique is the focus on how is welfare reform lived in smaller cities.

Research commenced in February 1998 when I trained as a shelter volunteer, learning to carry out the following tasks:

advocate for women at the Department of Social Services and Family Court; obtain orders of protection; answer hotline calls; and support women in their decisions to leave a battering situation. Although I missed one session, I completed the training course and began volunteering in March 1998. The first five months were startling, as I was sometimes unprepared for the physical manifestations of women's victimization. For instance, one day I entered the living room in the shelter and saw one of the residents, Diane, who was wearing a pair of shorts. My eyes were immediately drawn to a hole in her leg received from a gunshot wound by her ex-boyfriend. At first women in the shelter were uninterested in being interviewed by me. But after five months, I became more integrated into shelter life and accompanied women to appointments at the Department of Social Services, attended monthly staff meetings and client-based workshops, and went with women in search of apartments and jobs. While these activities fall under the rubric of participant observation, one of the methodological hallmarks of anthropology, this does not mean that my access to women's lives was unrestricted. I was unable to participate in every meeting women had due to the confidential nature of some sessions (such as therapeutic sessions). Also, on any given day, different women had overlapping appointments to keep, and I could not accompany each one. But I did accompany many women to the River Valley Department of Social Services (RVCDSS), where I was able to engage in in-depth discussions with them because the wait to see caseworkers often lasted several hours.

I also conducted formal structured interviews with the women during which they were asked to describe the incident that had precipitated their entry into the shelter. These initial interviews segued into life history interviews, the third method employed to understand battered women's experiences. Life history interviews are an excellent method for capturing feelings, attitudes, and events that have shaped women's experiences (Green-Powell 1997; Bozzoli 1991). Shostak (1989) notes that the life history method is an "elegant tool to describe the human condition. Ordinary people living ordinary and not-so-ordinary lives weave from their memories and experiences the meaning life has for them . . . they reveal the complexities and paradoxes of human life . . ." (Shostak 1989: 239).

Life histories were completed for 13 of the 22 women I interviewed. The discrepancy between the completed and incomplete interviews is a consequence of the fact that I did not always have enough time with women to finish the life histories. Whereas structured interviews took approximately one hour, life history interviews sometimes took up to 16 hours, and women did not always stay at the shelter long enough to meet with me for all or part of the follow-up interviews. I also suspect that some probably did not want to complete the interviews.

Other data collection methods included case record review. I obtained permission from most women to review their individual case file at the shelter. These contained legal documents, shelter staff notations and case updates, as well as summaries detailing women's activities, appointments, and progress in meeting goals.

Interviews were also conducted with 19 advocates representing six different community-based organizations, including Angel House Shelter. County personnel and staff employed at local institutions were interviewed as well. Among those interviewed were River Valley Department of Social Services administrators, the director of the Office of Section 8 Housing, supervisors at the Department of Labor, and some staff at the River Valley County Economic Development Corporation. In all 62 interviews were conducted, and field notes were kept in seven notebooks.

With regard to data analysis I tried to make the process "public" and did not do it in the "privacy of my head" as Salzinger (1997) notes she did. I created interpretive communities as part of the data analysis process, which involved discussing themes with individuals who were part of the study. As themes emerged during my manual coding process, I asked some of the people interviewed to participate in the interpretation or elaboration of those themes. For example, based on my coding of strategies that women used to address inadequate access to material goods, one woman was asked to read a summary of strategies I had prepared. She drew my attention to how women used "talk" as a way to get what they needed. I reviewed the data again and found that a number of women, in fact almost all of the Black women, engaged in this practice of talking to secure housing, food, and other necessities. Her observation and analysis became the section titled "Speech Acts," a discussion of which is found in chapter 8. Study participants were also solicited to review rough drafts of sections, especially if they were the focus of that chapter. This methodological strategy was my attempt to elaborate what it means to "do feminist ethnography," that is, to decrease the power imbalance between the researcher and those being researched (see Stacey 1988).

I cast this book as a feminist ethnography for two reasons. First because it privileges women's stories, and second my goal in writing it was to effect change in welfare reform policy. The first goal was accomplished on a practical level in the process of composing the ethnography, which often started with a woman's story the narrative around which the analysis emerged. It is for this reason that so much of women's words are presented all at once. Therefore, the reader will find lengthy quotes by women. The writing style moves between objectivity and subjectivity, between insertion of myself as ethnographer and more distanced interpretation. While this may be jarring, it represents the struggle of being an insider and an outsider and of having my heart in two places. As an insider, some of the women whom I interviewed had experiences echoing my own, and since my heart lies with them, my impulse is to not subject their lives to interpretation. But as an outsider, I am also part of the academy that I both embrace and resist because it is a space of intellectual and language production, which confuses academics and nonacademics, alike. I both admire and distrust this space, but as I attempt to negotiate it here, I try not to speak only in "another mother tongue," one that would be inaccessible to the women who appear in this ethnography, were they to read it. Therefore, I experiment with informality and formality, and move between storytelling and analysis, sometimes distinguished by an ornament, but other times not.

I hope that as a "woman writing culture," others reading culture, like those women whose stories are shared, and people who need to know those stories (like policymakers), find this work readable and that I have kept my promise to write in a way that does not require an English-to-English translation (see Behar and Gordon 1995). As a politically engaged anthropologist, it is my hope this ethnography can be used toward the larger goal of amending the devolution of social support and protections (Davis 2003).

Most women and shelter agency staff interviewed had little concern about me using their real names, and in fact only three people actually gave me pseudonyms to use. The others I simply made up drawing from my circle of friends and family members. I thought long and hard about whether or not to use the real name of the research site because the purpose of writing this book was not just to share women's experiences but also to effect changes in policies that are harmful to women. In the end I chose not to, because it occurred to me that some of the women whose lives are shared could be recognized. To maintain the location's anonymity, I do not list any source that would give it away. All statistics on the community come from the U.S. Census (1990–2000), U.S. Department of Housing and Urban Development (1995), U.S. Department of Labor (1990–2001), and City of "Laneville" websites, newspapers, and reports. In order to conceal the true identity of the city, figures and identifying data have been slightly altered. This decision was made because I also wanted to protect the relationships that community workers have or are trying to forge with the River Valley County Department of Social Service.

From Beginning to End

Beginning with a chapter titled "Three Women," the lives of three women, two who are Black and one who is White, are shared. Their stories reveal the circumstances of how they came to receive public assistance and demonstrate both how complicated it is to be battered and how violence and welfare are linked. It is in this chapter that the biographical sketches of the other women in the study are also presented.

Chapter 2 underscores the long-standing regulatory nature of welfare since its inception in the United States in 1935. The point of "Regulating Women" is to illustrate the ways that welfare has controlled and directed all women, but Black women in particular. This chapter historicizes welfare programs, explicates the new welfare law, and discusses the literature that has linked welfare and domestic violence. It rests on the axis of race, bringing into sharp relief just how critical race has been and is to the issue of welfare policy.

The stage for this ethnography is set in chapter 3, "Oh Sister, Shelter Me." Here I describe the two sites of engagement where women negotiated their lives. It begins with a brief history of Laneville and moves into a broader discussion of the emergence of battered women's shelters, specifically Angel House.

Following this is "Ceremonies of Degradation," where two case studies serve as a window into women's institutional relationship with the Department of Social Services and specifically portrays the tense interactions women have with caseworkers who are gatekeepers determining, confirming, or sometimes rejecting women's eligibility for assistance. What begins as control at the caseworker-client level of interaction moves along a path of increasing complexity, as women are given directives to meet the mandates of welfare reform. Chapters 5, 6, and 7 examine three other dimensions of Black women's experiences in relation to welfare reform: mandatory work and education, mothering and childcare, and housing. Chapter 5, "No Magic In The Market," examines the impact of deindustrialization in River Valley County on women's mandatory work and training options. Manufacturing work has been replaced by a burgeoning service economy, which tends to require unskilled or low-skilled workers. Since Blacks are disproportionately concentrated in service sector jobs and many approved welfare reform training programs prepare people for those positions, welfare reform has particular racialized implications. "The Theater of Maternal and Child Care Politics," chapter 6, offers three case studies illustrating the conflict of mothering within the context of welfare reform policy and the racial differences in support of mothering by social service caseworkers. In chapter 7, "There's No Place (Like Home)," we see the difficulties Black women have securing housing, in part due to the racialization of space and the impact of the processes of deindustrialization and gentrification.

While the overarching theme of this ethnography is how control prevails in understanding relations and transactions embedded in welfare reform policy, it is in chapter 8 that women's resistance takes center stage. The final chapter, "Strategic Missions," illustrates the attempts of Black women who are battered to defy and navigate being regulated by policy. Black feminist theory argues that Black women's oppressions must be contextualized by forms of resistances and resilience (Collins 1990). Thus, attention is focused on those resistive strategies women develop in the face of limited resources resulting from new policies and shifts in the local economy. Their resilience was often sandwiched between a rock and a hard place, and they did the best they could.

1

Three Women

Contemporary research suggests that Black women experience violence to a greater degree than other women, that they are more vulnerable to control by the state, and that they make up the largest percentage of women on welfare, although not the highest number. This percentage is in relation to the total number of Black women in the general population, for they do not comprise the largest number of women receiving assistance. Further concentrations of Black women on welfare are geographically specific in cities like New York, and they are at much greater risk of nonlethal,[1] intimate violence. Black women's reported rates of intimate partner violence are 35 percent higher than White females' reported rates, and Rennison and Welchans (2000) found that Black women report intimate partner violence at a rate 22 percent higher than women of other races/ethnicities.

We know that there are more reports of victimization for Black women than for White women, and we know that Black women are overrepresented among those who are poor, so it is crucial to explore the particularized experience of violence, race, and poverty. Interestingly, few studies examining the intersection of welfare and domestic abuse specifically incorporate race, which constitutes an important part of this ethnography given that data on violence and poverty point to the level of Black women's victimization.

Since women use welfare for a multitude of reasons, including as an immediate strategy to deal with domestic

violence, this chapter is concerned with how three women, two
Black and one White, utilized welfare in order to separate from
their abusers. I should clearly state that while violence may not
be the *main reason* that women use welfare, it is one of many
and an important mediating factor that *helps* women extricate
themselves from violent situations and in forming new households. And, although welfare critics view Black women on
welfare as lazy cheats, they have neither met Black women like
Sherita or Clemmie, nor imagined White women like Jocelyn,
whose stories are retold below.

Sherita

When we first met in the summer of 1998, Sherita's nose was
broken and one eye was stitched up. She had been attempting
to leave a battering relationship since early 1998 and was the
first Black woman at Angel House who legitimized my presence, and encouraged other Black women to talk to me. We
laughed, took long walks, and shopped for food for nearly two
years. Sherita shared the details of her life with me because she
said she wanted people to understand the constraints of pick-
ing up the pieces after having left a battering relationship in
the midst of welfare reform.

Sherita comes from a working-class family and was raised
in New York City with her brothers Mike and Andre. Her
father was a factory worker and her mother a homemaker. She
had a "good childhood, was well fed, well clothed and really
didn't want for anything."

When she was in her early teens Sherita's parents divorced,
and her mother struggled to make ends meet as a single parent
with little financial assistance from her ex-husband. Consequently Sherita's mother was on welfare for a total of 3 years,
which Sherita said meant her mother endured three years of
being looked down upon. Sherita finds this both ironic and
amusing, because her mother presently works for the New York
State Department of Social Services as a social worker.

Sherita completed high school and went to community college for one year. Although she had been looking forward to attending a four-year college along with her friends, her mother and grandmother did not want her far from home. Instead at age 19 she dated and married her best friend's brother, Lawrence. The first 17 years of the marriage were fine. Sherita worked as an administrative assistant for a small company, and even though Lawrence sometimes drank and gambled, they had money in the bank and a "very nicely furnished apartment." Sherita neither drank nor gambled; she was family-oriented and really wanted to maintain a positive home environment. She loved Lawrence, and the two of them were wrapped in a cocoon of family activities, having dinner with their families on weekends and making annual sojourns down South every summer for Lawrence's family reunions.

Things soured during the last two years of their marriage when Lawrence began staying out all night and spending money recklessly. They fought, and while he was not physically abusive, his irresponsibility grated on Sherita's nerves. She was not interested in "going down"—she had worked too hard. In 1997 Sherita ended the marriage: "I had finally had it with my drunken, gambling husband. I realized he was not going to grow up after 19 years of being together. I left him knowing it would be hard and knowing that I would be alone, which is something I never was. I started my new life in a new location."

The new location turned out to be the town of Valencia in River Valley County, near Laneville, where her brother Mike had moved several years before, after his marriage to Elena. She lived with Mike and his wife for a few months, planning to leave after saving some money. Almost immediately Sherita was hired in a long-term temporary position at Zytron Corporation, as an administrative assistant with no health benefits. She drove to the office each day and took her lunch to save money. Things went well for several months, and then for reasons Sherita still does not understand, Mike's wife, Elena, began to make her feel very unwelcome. Elena's coldness and

Mike's unwillingness to mediate drove a deep wedge between Mike and Elena, and Sherita. The wedge was so deep that after her car broke down and she was unable to get it repaired, Sherita refused to ask Mike or Elena for any assistance, sensing her request would be turned down.

Zytron was a 25-minute drive from the house, but Mike never offered to give her a lift, leaving Sherita to rely on public transportation. The limited bus system in River Valley County meant that by the time Sherita got off from work there were no buses going back to Valencia. However, a friendship forged with a woman on the job was Sherita's saving grace, allowing her get to and from work. Although Sherita asked little of her brother and his wife, tension continued to mount: "I would come home at night, hungry after a hard day's work. There would be Elena in the kitchen cleaning the oven or mopping the floor, at like 11:00 p.m. She was going out of her way to make me unwelcome. That's why I moved into a rooming house. That's where I met Joey."

After moving to the rooming house in early 1998, Sherita met Joey. They were drawn to each other, she said, out of loneliness. Joey was on medical leave from his job with the commuter railroad and did little to pass the time. At first they just kept each other company, and over time Joey convinced Sherita to live with him in his room so that they could save money together. But shortly after the move, Joey began to use cocaine. Things grew worse when Sherita was no longer able to depend upon the woman who drove her to and from work, and she resigned from her job. Being unemployed and living with a drug user frightened Sherita, particularly as Joey increasingly threatened her and became physically abusive.

In need of emergency assistance, Sherita went to the River Valley County Department of Social Services located in Laneville, about 20 minutes from Valencia. Her goal was to access their job placement services, secure food stamps, housing, and cash assistance so she could leave Joey. Sherita filed for food stamps, but was told it would take several weeks to approve her application. A job counselor sent her on several interviews, at jobs that did not pay a living wage, nor did they draw upon her administrative assistant skills. However, Sherita's stick-to-itiveness paid off, and she landed another temporary job as a secretary. This job, like many in River Valley, was located in an area with an inadequate transportation system, but she was able to get to work on the weekdays. What she could not do was get to work on the weekend, and when she was called in to work one Sunday, Sherita was unable to get to the office and was fired. Because she had been fired, which her caseworker assumed was her fault, Sherita was told she would not be able to access assistance for three months.

> I couldn't get to the job because of transportation reasons. When I went back to RVCDSS to get emergency funds, they said I wasn't eligible because I refused to work. But that was not true. I couldn't work. The job called for me to work on Sunday and they needed me on Sunday, but I couldn't get there. RVCDSS sanctioned me for 90 days, so I couldn't get any food stamps or nothing.

In addition to not receiving benefits, Sherita experienced an escalation in Joey's drug use and threatening behavior.

> I noticed things he would do like go into the bathroom and stay there. Or if I gave him what little money I had, I wondered "why isn't there any food?" He couldn't hide it no more. He would give me money to hold and before the night was out, he would want the money back. He belittled me a lot, saying stuff like 'I'm the one giving you a place to stay.' Or, one minute we could be talking like you and I right now, sitting across from each other. He'd be getting high; he'd be calm, cool and collected. And then he would snap. I might go into the bathroom and he'd follow me, close the door and next thing I know I'm on the floor. He'd be holding on to my neck screamin' at me 'WHOSE TAKIN' CARE OF YOU?' I had to get out of the apartment.

The next month she moved out of their shared room and went to live with her neighbors; she also returned to social services and revised her application, this time checking off the box indicating she was a victim of domestic violence. The new welfare law had an amendment, the Family Violence Option, which should have facilitated Sherita's ability to access services. In spite of this protective measure, she was not flagged as being a victim of domestic violence by the caseworker and was denied assistance due to having been fired:

> I go back to RVCDSS and see this worker [a different one than the one she had seen before]. I forget her name. She started off by being nice to me. But when we got to her office she turned on me. She said to me 'So you can't keep a job?' [She was referring to the job that Sherita had lost]. I said to her, 'It must be that file, it's all wrong.' I said to her, 'If we're going to talk about that, I might as well leave.' I knew the sanction and the job thing was in that file. But I'm more than that file.
>
> We never talked about why I was there or that I checked the box saying I was in a violent relationship. I mean I had checked the box on the form and she just didn't pick up on it. All we talked about was the job I was let go from. So I had to tell her I was homeless living in some people's apartment in order to get some emergency help.

Because she was homeless, the caseworker sent Sherita to the RVCDSS housing counselor, who put her up in a motel and helped her locate a place to live. But given that she was sanctioned, Sherita was ineligible for cash benefits, food stamps, or housing cost assistance. With no job and only abbreviated assistance from RVCDSS, locating an apartment was meaningless because there was no way to pay the rent. Of her own volition Sherita found a job that she could get to by bus, working as a cashier at a discount store making $120 a week before taxes. The pay was not much, but it was all she could get. Her plan was to wait until the sanction from Social Services was lifted—two more months. When the time came, she would reapply for housing assistance. Until then, Sherita continued to stay at her neighbors' apartment and hoped Joey would not bother her, which of course he did.

After the 3-month sanction period ended, in July of 1998, Sherita again went to RVCDSS for emergency assistance. This time she was given a budget of $350 for an apartment, and was provided with rental listings from which she found a place to live. Social Services had to approve the apartment before permitting her to move in, and it was just a matter of a week or so before she could do so. In that time, Joey beat Sherita, as she explained, "almost beyond recognition." If only they had provided assistance before, she may not have been beaten.

Sherita came to the shelter seeking safety and discovered she had to file for benefits again, since in New York State, shelters are paid a per diem rate for each resident through reimbursement from the Department of Social Services. This time, she went with a shelter advocate who informed the same caseworker Sherita had most recently seen that Sherita had previously checked the box for domestic violence on her application. The caseworker said Sherita had not done so. But when she looked down at the application, she realized she had overlooked the notation. The caseworker looked scared, according to Sherita, and apologized profusely. As Sherita later told me, "I think I could have sued them for what happened. There is a woman on site at RVCDSS especially for that [the Domestic Violence Liaison] and I never got to see her." The caseworker's apology was too late. Sherita's nose was broken, and one eye was swollen shut. Joey had punched Sherita in the mouth, dislodged several of her teeth and split her lip. On her shelter intake form was the following notation: *"She has injuries from the beating that will need further attention."* The attention required was, in fact, surgery.

With her application approved Sherita received Medicaid, a housing stipend, food stamps, and cash benefits through Safety Net funding, the program for single adults without children. However, the apartment that had been found was now gone, and Sherita searched and found another for $500 into which she moved in November of 1998, 3 months after arriving at the shelter. Sherita initiated her relationship with Social Services for two overlapping reasons: lack of resources and the need to get away from Joey. With a job that paid so little, there was no way for her to secure an apartment. Sherita had been at risk of bodily harm, and, in her estimation, only welfare could help save her life.

Clemmie

Clemmie is a 38-year-old African-American woman who prior to coming to Angel House lived in an apartment in New York City with her four children; two daughters, Shawnice, 19, and Lena, 18; and two sons, James and Henry, who are 15 and 9, respectively.

A few days after we met at the shelter, right around Thanksgiving I was asked to pick Clemmie up at a train station. She had to come into New York City to access her cash and food stamps electronically from the New York City Department of Human Resources. After three attempts, we found a place that would dispense her benefits, and I then offered to drive Clemmie and Shawnice back up to the shelter. Although it was cold, it was a beautiful fall day, a good day for a relaxing drive with a woman on the run. Clemmie seemed relieved she would not have to go back to Laneville on the train. It was too open, and she feared seeing someone she knew. Shawnice settled in the back seat, pulled her coat over her head and fell asleep. This ride began a one-and-a-half-year relationship during which Clemmie shared her life story with me.

Clemmie grew up in a family of five children. She and her siblings Doreatha, Jake, Sonia, and Angie, all lived with their mother. When Clemmie was 16, her mother became ill and sent the kids to live with Clemmie's eldest sister, Doreatha, who became a "mother" to Clemmie and her siblings. Doreatha, who worked in the finance industry, was financially stable and moved her brothers and sisters into her home on Long Island, where they all lived comfortably. Because Clemmie was such a responsible young woman, she was elevated to the role of coparent. She was the only person with house keys—none of the others were given a set of keys; they all had to organize their arrival at home according to Clemmie's schedule. Yet no one ever had to worry; when Clemmie said she would be home, she'd be there. Very little that would qualify as exciting happened in the three years Clemmie lived with Doreatha. But at age 19, Clemmie became pregnant and not wanting to burden Doreatha, moved to a Section 8 apartment, where she lived for 19 years until she was forced to leave due to violence.

Clemmie's first three children all have the same father, Allan, with whom she had a long-term relationship. Eventually they grew apart, and Clemmie met someone else, Tony, who is the father of her youngest son, Henry. Although no longer with either man, Clemmie negotiated regular visits between her children and their fathers. Allan saw Shawnice, Lena, and James regularly. Tony, Henry's father, was not as reliable but did visit occasionally. Without a full-time partner, Clemmie did an excellent job raising her children, taking them on day trips and exposing them to cultural events. Clemmie instilled the importance of education in her children, spending considerable time working with them on their homework and fostering their interests. The children were very bright, including Shawnice, who had had dropped out of high school only because she was bored. Lena, an exceptionally bright young woman, had been awarded a full scholarship to an elite high school and then went on to receive a full scholarship to a private university. James was also an "A" student, and Henry was a gifted child, although challenged by asthma. It was Henry's asthma that precipitated Clemmie applying for social services. She had worked in construction and in retail sales, but Henry's day-care provider kept calling her away from work because of asthma attacks. Knowing that she would be fired as a result of missing too many work days, she left her job and applied for social services. This was fine with her because she could care

for the kids herself and keep them "on the right track." They
were all independent, well-adjusted, and were close to Clemmie's siblings, whom they visited every weekend. By most
accounts, one might say her children's successes challenge
stereotypical ideas about poor women and bad Black mothers.

Clemmie was the center of her children's life and they,
hers. But as the children grew older, they did not need her as
much as they once did, and Clemmie felt something was missing in her life. This was her explanation as to why she became
involved with an abusive man. She wanted to be with someone
who needed her, a man whose name she never mentioned the
entire time we knew each other. She only referred to him as her
"batterer" or, "he." As we drove back to Laneville, Clemmie
told me how she came to the shelter. In a soft voice she said:

> I've known him for quite some time, almost 12 years.
> We had been friends and we saw each other around
> the way. We started hanging out together about a
> year ago. In the beginning he was very nice. He
> would invite me over and we would go to the movies.
> He would get tickets for my boys to go to basketball
> games. But within the last three months, he's been
> really obsessive, yelling at me in the street, pushing
> me.

Clemmie was terribly afraid that "he" would harm her or her
children. He was abusive in front of her childrens' friends. One
evening he held a gun to Clemmie's head taunting Shawnice's
friends, asking if they wanted to see him blow her head off.
But more than her own safety, she feared the threats he made
to her family and friends:

> I told my family about him, and everybody was afraid
> of what he was going to do. He scared my children.
> So it got to the point that when he would come over
> and ring my bell, I'd put on my clothes, meet him
> downstairs and tell him I was just on the way to his
> house and we would leave. That way he wouldn't do

anything in front of the kids. He started checking up
on me, calling my "mother's" house to make sure I
was there. He couldn't call me at home 'cause he
never knew I had a phone. Whenever he would come
over, I would hide the phone, so he never knew. He's
got friends who work for Social Services. He always
knew when I got my food stamps or my check and
would come over asking for money. His friend would
tell him. That's why I had to use my benefit card
someplace else, so he wouldn't be able to trace me.
That's why I needed you to pick me up so he wouldn't
know where I was living by where I used my card.

The more Clemmie tried to get out of the relationship, the
more violent he became. She visited friends for long periods, so
"he" could not find her. One of her sisters had to move, so
that "he" wouldn't continue to harass her about where Clemmie was. Other family members, including her "mother," told
her not to call "until this whole thing got straight," and her
younger sister Angie, who lived in the same neighborhood as
"he" did, put up a pretense of hating Clemmie, aligning herself
with him so he wouldn't hurt Angie or her children.

Clemmie and the children came to Angel House in the fall
of 1998 because "he" had asked her to sell some drugs, and
she refused. Her refusal sparked a violent tirade. To keep dis-
tance between the two of them, she decided not to answer any
knocks on the door.

A couple of nights after he asked me to sell, me and
all the kids were at home and he come banging on
the door. I told the kids to be quiet so he wouldn't
know we were there. He was screaming at the door
for me to let him in and he was trying to break it
down. Finally the building security called the police
and they came to take him away. When they did, he
was yelling 'Bitch I'm gonna kill you and your kids.' I
called Victims Services, a number my sister gave me.
They told me there was room up here, [at Angel

House] so we got on the train with no money. I had to ask the conductor to let us on for free and we came up here in the middle of the night.

Clemmie's story contradicts the public identity of welfare mothers. While many are portrayed as lazy, Clemmie worked throughout her children's formative years and only first accessed welfare as a way to care for her sick son. But also her ability to stay home and raise her children the way she saw fit contributed to their achievements, in her eyes. Her continued need for welfare was specifically in relation to the abuse, and she now needed support in order to establish a safe home.

Jocelyn

Jocelyn is a middle-class White woman, who came to the shelter after an "accident" involving Gus, her husband of one year. We sat outside on a beautiful fall day, as Jocelyn told me what happened to her and how she ended up at the shelter.

I was born in a small town in Virginia. The house I grew up in had a lot of land surrounding it which is the reason I love nature. As a child I spent quite a bit of time catching caterpillars and watching their transformations; I was mesmerized. I loved nature and the outdoors so much. I also loved to ride horses. There was such a sense of freedom riding horses that I begged my parents to let me take lessons at the stables near our house.

It was at the stables that she met her first husband and the father of her two children, Joshua, age 20, and Jenny, age 13. The other thing Jocelyn loved to do was paint. "I love to draw nature scenes, leaves, trees and flowers. She [her daughter] doesn't paint as much I did. I was really good at it, but I probably won't be able to do it anymore, with all this nerve damage." Jocelyn looked sad as she reflected on how the injuries she had sustained would limit her life. If only she had not left Virginia, had not moved to River Valley, New York, she might not have met Gus.

In early July, Jocelyn was in a "motorcycle accident," at least that is what she told me when I did her intake. The "accident" involved Gus, Jocelyn's husband, who walked away with a scratch on his arm, while she ended up in the hospital with her jaw wired shut, head trauma, dilated eyes, a broken arm and jaw, nerve damage, and seizures.

One reason no one at the shelter really believed there had been a motorcycle accident was that hospital personnel, in collaboration with another battered women's program telephoned the Angel House hotline on Jocelyn's behalf to see if there was any room available for her. When we said yes, Jocelyn's hospital discharge was conducted in secrecy; she had to be sneaked out of the hospital because Gus had been stalking Jocelyn during her recovery. Many of us at the shelter believed that he stalked her as a form of intimidation to prevent Jocelyn from telling anyone the truth; that Gus had beaten her and that was the reason she ended up in the hospital. Although Jocelyn did not give me access to her medical report, I believe that there is a difference between the type of injury associated with a beating than those associated with road rash.

Gus was a police officer whom Jocelyn had known for a year before they married. He was charming and handsome, she said. Gus wanted Jocelyn to be a homemaker, but Jocelyn had other plans. Although Jocelyn had graduated from high school, she decided to go back to school and earn a college degree. She asked Gus to pay for her classes, which she did not think would be a problem. After all, he made about $50,000–$60,000 (with overtime) a year and owned the house they lived in, which was almost paid off. Gus refused.

Jocelyn wanted to attend school so badly that she took a job cleaning homes to earn the money. Around this same period, Gus began to be very intimidating, illustrating the response that abusers often have when women exert their autonomy. Through wired teeth, Jocelyn told me how Gus increasingly frightened her, yelling if she looked at him, for example. Or, at other times, she said "If he didn't like what I cooked, he would squeeze my face so hard my jaws would ache." Sometimes Jocelyn, Jenny, and Gus were all watching television, and Gus would just ball up his fist, and shake it in Jocelyn's face. Gus often grabbed Jocelyn so hard that the imprint of his hands would cause bruising on her arm.

Gus's abuse was not limited to Jocelyn. On several occasions he pinned Jenny up against the wall by holding her arms above her head. He also directed random outbursts toward Jenny that frightened her so much she no longer brought her friends over to the house. After each incident, Gus would say he did not remember doing anything to either Jocelyn or Jenny. Jocelyn decided it was time for them to leave the house before things got any worse. Shortly after that decision was made, the "motorcycle accident" occurred.

Completing Jocelyn's intake included making a copy of her identification. She asked me to look in her wallet for her license, which I did. As I pulled it out, she said, "I used to look good. That photo was taken a year ago." It was startling how different Jocelyn looked sitting in front of me, than how she appeared in the photograph. The license photograph showed a smiling, cheerful woman. But sitting before me, at that moment she appeared much older than her 37 years with circles under her eyes and a drawn in face, a shadow of a person; Jocelyn had been slowly beaten down.

Jocelyn had no source of income, now that she was no longer living with Gus and was unable to work. She was not eligible for unemployment because she had been working off the books cleaning houses. Jocelyn needed welfare because she had no source of income, although on paper as Gus's wife, she might be considered middle-class. She told me that when she applied to RVCDSS, she was treated with disdain. "They treated me like a leper because I am not considered poor. I am. I don't have anything right now. I hate them for treating me so badly." Jocelyn felt that she challenged the perception of who was supposed to be getting social services, because she was a middle-class White woman. Caseworkers seemed silently offended that she betrayed the privilege of whiteness by having to apply for assistance. Despite the fact that her caseworker seemed disillusioned that a woman like Jocelyn would have to apply for assistance, she processed the application and directed her to see Yvonne, the Domestic Violence Liaison. Yvonne exempted Jocelyn from having to work for two months, so she could heal. This was quite a different outcome from Sherita's treatment, who also needed to heal, but was never directed to the Domestic Violence Liaison. Also, an appointment was made for Jocelyn to meet with the RVCDSS housing specialist, and an apartment was found just outside of Laneville in a predominantly White neighborhood within 30 days of her being admitted to the shelter. Whereas Jocelyn was at the shelter for about 1 month before she secured housing, most of the Black women stayed a full 90 days, the maximum amount of time allotted for shelter stay.

Sherita, Clemmie, and Jocelyn are three women who were in no way abusing the welfare system. Collectively their experiences show that they were neither lazy nor unmotivated. In fact their stories point to two important ways that welfare helped women. On the one hand, it served as unemployment compensation for women at the low end of the labor market, as in Sherita and Jocelyn's case. On the other hand, it facilitated being able to stay home with children, which often leads to better social outcomes, as was the case with Clemmie. Their needs and reasons for using welfare were very similar to the women whose biographies are provided below. The differences between them, however, and their entanglements with the welfare bureaucracy and the struggle to find and create homes are complicated by race.

Biographical Sketches

Sherita, Clemmie, and Jocelyn are three of the women I met at Angel House shelter for battered women. Biographical sketches of all 22 women formally interviewed are presented below, but these capsule summaries represent very condensed versions of much longer life histories. Contained in these abbreviated translations, we see some of the shocking details that defined these women's engagement with the social welfare system. While these women do not represent all battered women, the distinctiveness of their experiences can provide insight into battered women's needs, as they tried to establish different lives from the ones they had.

Throughout this book are the names of other women, including community residents and professionals like community-based and institutional personnel, but here I only provide biographical sketches of the battered women living at the shelter from whom I collected substantial data, since this book is primarily about their experiences. Those who are discussed at length in subsequent chapters are noted here with an asterisk. Some of the women I spoke with are not discussed in detail or even referred to, and there are other women I met whose biographies are not included, but to whom I refer in the book. However, I want to emphasize the importance of each woman's experience, and that all of the women and people I interviewed contributed to my understanding of the issues raised.

Angela is originally from Spain. She is 35 and was married to a nuclear physicist. The household income was over $75,000 per year. She has one son Elmo, 13, and one daughter Eugenia, age 16, from two other relationships. She has never received public assistance and at the time I interviewed her, she still was not getting assistance. Angela and her husband met during his vacation in her native Spain. He pursued her and ultimately convinced her to move to the United States with her children and marry him. He isolated Angela and would not allow her to work. She left him after he exposed himself to her daughter.

*Clemmie** is a 38-year-old African-American woman with four children. Her daughters Shawnice and Lena are 19 and 18, respectively. Her two sons, James and Henry are 15 and 9, respectively. Clemmie became involved with a man who threatened her constantly and alienated her from her family, forcing her to flee to River Valley County.

Drita is a 60-year-old woman from Eastern Europe. She has five adult children and many grandchildren. She left her husband because he had beaten her for almost 40 years. She does not speak English very well, and although she is a legal permanent resident, has had tremendous difficulty in securing any type of benefits.

Elizabeth*, who is 39, was born in Jamaica. She has dual citizenship in the United States and Great Britain. She has two children by her husband, whom she met in college. She has been separated from him for almost four years because he was abusive. She went on public assistance after the birth of her youngest child who, at birth, was hospitalized for almost a month. This same child seems to have learning disabilities as well as severe asthma.

Gloria* is a 40-year-old African-American woman who has several children. She has had an alcohol abuse problem for much of her life and had been at the battered women's shelter several times before I met her there. She was beaten and thrown out of an apartment she shared with a boyfriend.

Iliana* is 32 years old. Iliana is an Afro-Latina, born in the Dominican Republic. She came to the United States at the age of 18. Iliana has three children and had just given birth to the third child when we met. The father of the two oldest children was emotionally and verbally abusive to her, so she left him. The father of her third child also "showed signs of being abusive," so she ended their relationship.

Jennifer is a single African-American, 23-year-old woman who graduated from high school and now works in children's services. Jennifer grew up with both her parents and a sister. Although her father was strict and her parents separated when she was 11, Jennifer says she has a good relationship with both of them. Jennifer has been living on her own since she was 18. She had been with her boyfriend for just about a year when she came to the shelter. Jennifer was very independent and did not need him for money, which she believes, is the reason that he beat her.

*Joanne** is a 28-year-old African-American mother. She has one child, a boy named JD, 5 years old, and is pregnant with her second child. Joanne grew up in a middle-class home. Her father was a minister, and her mother, a homemaker. She was sexually and physically abused by her father and was placed in a group home at age 15. At 18 Joanne attended community college, where she met the father of her children. When they first met, he was very good to her and only later in the relationship did he become abusive and jealous.

*Jocelyn** is a 36-year-old White woman who grew up in Virginia. She has two children, one 20, and the other 13. Her husband, Gus, who is not the father of her children, constantly made threatening remarks to her and the youngest daughter who lived with them. Jocelyn feared for her life, as her husband became increasingly abusive.

Joelle is a 20–year-old, African-American woman, originally from Madison, Wisconsin. As a child, Joelle was adopted and experienced sexual assault five days per week from the age of 5 to 8. "It was always in the house, a cousin, an adopted sibling—someone." Joelle graduated from high school, and went on to college, but left due to financial constraints. Joelle came to Laneville and met a guy who beat her almost all the time.

*Josie** is a young, White woman in her 20s with one daughter, Shaneva. Shaneva's father, Luke, had promised to marry Josie, but the wedding never took place. Josie left Luke because he was trying to control her every move and had begun to hit her.

Khadija is a 19-year-old, Muslim woman born to parents who immigrated from India. Her parents are very strict and try to keep a tight rein on Khadija, who attends college. They sometimes follow her to and from school to try and prevent her from seeing the young African-American man she is dating. Her parents despise him and sometimes severely punish her when Khadija does not act according to their wishes. Khadija came to the shelter because of the violence her parents perpetrate against her.

*Leslie** is a 19-year-old, pregnant, African-American woman. She has an estranged relationship with her mother who used to beat her, but came to the shelter because her boyfriend became abusive shortly after she found out she was pregnant.

Linda is a 19-year-old Black woman from the Caribbean, with one son. She is estranged from her family because they abused her. Linda was never able to access social services because of her immigrant status. Her parents and her boyfriend battered her. While at the shelter, she was depressed and had gynecological health problems that made it very difficult to do any kind of planning for her departure from the shelter.

Martha is a 19-year-old, African-American woman who lived most of her life in foster care during which time she was sexually abused. She arrived in Laneville from Chicago with a young man, Andre, she had met while there. Andre turned out to be a drug dealer and used her to sell drugs from the motel they lived in. One night they were stopped by police officers, after which Andre beat her. She left him just after the beating.

Michelle is a 22-year-old mother of one. She is Black/Hispanic and grew up in Brooklyn in a working-class family. Although her father used drugs, her mother kept the family financially solvent. Growing up, Michelle recalls being on social services only for a short period, when her father was unemployed for about a year. The father of Michelle's child, Al, was a drug dealer and user. On at least one occasion she cooperated with the police to have Al arrested.

Sherita * is a single, African-American, 38-year-old woman. She grew up living with her mother, stepfather, and two brothers. Sherita was married at age 19 and left her husband after 19 years due to his gambling and drinking problem. Her batterer is someone she met after she moved to Laneville. She began using social services shortly after he started beating her.

Solange * is a 42-year-old African-American mother of 2 children. She takes pride in the fact that she was able to complete college and has worked in the social services field for most of her adult life. Solange's husband is economically dependent upon her because he is functionally illiterate and cannot hold a job. She believes he beats her because of his own sense of inadequacy and has caused her to seek shelter at least five times.

Susan is a 36-year-old White woman with 6 children. She has worked primarily in the service industry at fast-food restaurants. Susan is illiterate, probably due to a learning disability that was never diagnosed. Her lack of literacy skills has limited her employment options to those that do not require her to read. Susan has been in and out of shelters since 1992 and recently crossed state lines to get away from her abuser. Susan has been very engaged with social service systems for most of her adult life ranging from child welfare agencies, the Division of Youth and Family Services, criminal court, family courts, and housing authorities.

Trudi * is in her 30s. She came to the United States from Ghana. She has one birth daughter and an "adopted" daughter, whom she and her husband Sam brought with them when they left Ghana. The husband has transformed the nature of his relationship with the "adopted" daughter so that she now is treated as a co-wife. Trudi is on social services while she is attending school to finish her Bachelor's degree in computer programming. Her husband has a full scholarship to a private college as well.

Wenny is a 42-year-old Chinese immigrant. She and her husband, who are legal permanent residents, have done well for themselves since immigrating, raising two children and owning a business. He recently began to threaten her and brandished a gun several times in front of the children. She went to court to secure an order of protection. While there, she saw some business clients (including the judge) and was devastated.

Yvonne is from South America. She is 37 and has two children, both of whom were born in the United States. At the time of our interview, her immigrant status was unclear. Yvonne's husband grossly mistreated the older child, who was not his, by locking him in closets and suspending him upside down when he misbehaved.

❧

Of the 22 women I spent time with over nearly 2 years, 13 were Black, 4 White, 3 Latina, 1 Asian, and 1 was Indian. The racial/ethnic breakdown of the overall shelter population was different than the study participants because I wanted to learn more about Black women's experiences. So, whereas 41% of the shelter residents were White, 33% were Black; 18% Latina, 2% Asian, and 7% identified as other, the breakdown of study participants is 18% White; 59% Black; 14% Latina, 5% Asian, and 5% identified as Other. Also, the average shelter resident had less than 12 years of education, but the average study participant had a high school diploma, some college, or vocational training.

Besides the inverted Black/White demographic, all other characteristics of the study participants and the general shelter population were comparable. The average study participant was between 30 and 39 years old and Black. Most of the women were single with children, and at the time of shelter entry most had household incomes of less than $9,999. Similarly, among the larger shelter population the average shelter resident was also between the ages of 30 and 39, and had a household income of less than $9,999.[2]

This ethnography amplifies Black women's experiences with comparisons made to White women. Black women are the focus of this book because much of what we understand about Black women who are battered is in terms of their use of public organizations (i.e. law enforcement and social services), and how racism factors into their hesitancy about reporting their victimization or reaching out to helping institutions (Powdermaker 1939; Websdale 2001; Garfield 2004). As you read on, you will see that after the women leave abusive relationships and are living in a shelter, they attempt to reestablish their lives. Their use of government assistance is crucial given that they live in a community that has undergone economic changes, especially shifts in labor as a result of deindustrialization. What becomes clear is that for these women, welfare reform's singular referent to "self-sufficiency," so narrowly defined in terms of attachment to work, brushes over the complexities of how communities are marked by the disappearance of jobs and the restructuring of labor markets, which exacerbate hierarchies, particularly racial ones. In many ways women are revictimized by welfare reform programs and policy within the context of economic restructuring, after having had the courage to leave their abusers.

2

Regulating Women's Lives

At its inception in 1935, the welfare state provided an infra-structure intended to "maintain families, the labor force and the general welfare of society" through the systematic redistribution of working people's income to those who were not employed (Abramovitz 1996: 215). The programs filled in as a substitute wage and were, to a limited degree, an effort to modify market forces and provide security for those whose income was interrupted by retirement, disability, widowhood, unemployment, or illness.[1] Legislating the various programs described below, was an expression of the government's concern and sentiment with prioritizing the care of its citizens. Out of economic disarray the Keynesian welfare state, as it is referred to, was congruent with an industrial society and supported the labor market through the defense of unions and greater wage equality. The programs included the Social Security Act, which established a national retirement system entitling primarily male workers to social security and unemployment insurance, and upon their deaths, their wives and children would receive the benefits. This program has been described as "dignified entitlement" because no proof or means tests were required to secure income support, since recipients were automatically entitled to their benefits by virtue of their participation in the labor force. The other components of the welfare state established in 1935 were categorical programs for the elderly, the sick, and aid for single mothers with children—the program known as Aid to Dependent Children

(ADC) (Handler 1995; Piven and Cloward 1993). These support programs have been described as "humiliating relief" because recipients had to prove that they qualified to receive income support. Proof of eligibility was particularly humiliating for single mothers receiving ADC, as they were subjected to degrading probes into their private lives in order to verify their entitlement. ADC only offered assistance to children lacking parental support as a result of death, long-term absence, or incapacity of the family (Gordon 1990; Abramovitz 1996). In this regard, ADC then was available to the children of primarily White widows or whose *married* parents were estranged or incapacitated.[2] This meant that the children of single, never-married women were ineligible—especially Black women, whose labor was an economic necessity. The racial organization of labor was realized in the South through ADC to accommodate Southern political leaders who insisted that states hold the right to establish eligibility for who should receive ADC benefits. Since the Southern economy depended on the labor of Black workers, receipt of benefits for them was severely circumscribed.

In 1962 ADC was revised, as another program titled Aid to Families with Dependent Children (AFDC) permitted women on welfare to do some work while at the same time receive benefits. Eligibility was also opened up to allow some two-parent families to receive welfare at this time, and states began providing a number of services to recipients. It was through accessing this program—AFDC—that the number of Black women receiving benefits began to increase.

Clearly the welfare state has been both a safety net and a system with practices, policies and programs that control and organize relations between individuals and the state. Here I define the state as the formal governmental system composed of legislative policymakers, regulatory entities, as well as those who carry out policies and regulations (Lubiano 1992). This chapter examines five ways in which welfare policies regulate, or at the very least influence, various aspects of social life, particularly at the intersection of race and gender. It explores how these intersections are articulated especially in the lives of

Black women and concludes with an overview of the Welfare Reform Act of 1996 and the links between welfare reform and violence against women.

One sphere regulated by welfare policy is labor markets (Piven 1999) and as both Quadagno (1994) and Mink (1990) point out, welfare policy has profoundly regulated Black people's labor since social programs were first instituted in 1935. A second domain linked to welfare is illuminated by Gordon (1994) and Abramovitz (1996), who both discuss how welfare has been viewed as an explanation for the disintegration of the Black family, due to Black women's utilization of programs. According to Piven and Cloward (1993), social welfare has historically regulated civil disorder, and as we will see, this tradition has been carried forward through the 1960s. A fourth area influenced by welfare policy is connected to the image of Black women, which according to Collins (1990) and Jewell (1993) has denigrated Black women by constructing them as the primary users of welfare programs. The last sphere that welfare factors into is the control over Black women's reproductive capabilities. Here Roberts' (1997) analysis is germane, as she delves into the policies that have been used to limit Black women's fertility.

Labor Market Regulation

Several scholars have astutely analyzed the regulation of labor markets through welfare (Piven and Cloward 1993; Nelson 1990). Labor markets are generally organized into three categories: 1) productive labor; 2) domestic labor; and 3) reproductive labor (Nelson 1990). The main concern here is productive labor. In the early stages of the welfare state, productive labor was structured to meet the needs of industrial society as well as the political, ideological, and economic interests of White men. For example, the provision of Social Security went to working men in mostly White, male-dominated industries. Agricultural laborers, private domestic servants, local state and federal government employees and workers in nonprofit, charitable, scientific, literary, and educational institutions were ineligible to receive unemployment insurance. The end result of these exclusions was that the welfare state was responsive primarily to White industrial workers. Social Security and Unemployment Insurance programs were discriminatory. A hierarchical order of privilege, which was both raced and gendered, constructed and maintained exclusion because most of the workers falling into the disqualified categories were White women, Black men, and Black women (Quadagno 1994). For Black women, who have historically filled what are viewed as low-level functions in the U.S. labor market, their vulnerability to poverty increased, as they were both relegated to the lowest wage-earning jobs (Harley 2002) and were barred from receiving government support.

Linking the Black Family to Poverty and Welfare Use

Among the reasons Black women were denied assistance was the nation's need for Black female labor, undermining the importance of Black maternalism and negating Black women's roles as homemakers. What was ironic was the fact that they worked was used against them in evaluating the validity of the Black family and its household structure. Consequently, negative constructions of the Black family were drawn from the transcript of Black women's participation in wage labor and as heads of households, framing the Black family as degenerate and disorganized. We see one articulation of this in a study on Southern Blacks by sociologist Dollard (1937) who noted:

> [The Negro woman's] economic independence puts her in a position to challenge the assumption of the strict patriarchal position by the Negro man. The family among lower-class Negroes seems, by and large to be a much less stable unit than in the White group, to exercise less coercive control over children, and to liberate them earlier for productive activity. (414)

Black women bore the blame for the sociologically constructed "depraved condition" of the Black family. In trying to understand the problems in the Black community, sociologist E. Franklin Frazier (1939) explained that the Black family and the transmission of African kinship and family relations had been destroyed by slavery. Among his findings was a lack of stability among Blacks, which he explained as a product of a matriarchal household structure. The problem with the Black family was that Black female heads of household had displaced male dominance. The currency of these claims, along with the need for Black labor, were central reasons for restricting Black women's receipt of assistance. In the 1930s Black exclusion from receipt of assistance prevailed in spite of the fact that nearly 50% of African Americans were unemployed and required social supports. Regardless of unemployment rates in 1935, only 15% of Black family heads were certified to receive public relief (Jewell 1993: 106; see also Skocpol 1988).

The continued practice of excluding Blacks from receiving assistance may be linked to the persistent vilification of the Black family, which nearly 30 years after Dollard and Frazier's arguments were resuscitated by Moynihan (1965). He reported that Black women's dominance in the family was counterintuitive to the normative patriarchal family, and hypothesized that matriarchal familial structure led to poverty, welfare, and a host of other social ills.

Revisions of the Black family and Black women's maternalism followed the civil rights movement. Studies illustrating the uniqueness and strength of the Black family and Black women have been undertaken by a number of scholars (see for example Ladner 1971; Mullings 1986; Hill 1999). One of the most instrumental studies challenging the pathology of the Black family is found in historian Herbert Gutman's (1976) study. He drew upon census data, birth records, and marriage applications to discern the structure of the Black family during slavery. Gutman found that the Black family was indeed based on a nuclear model, and that the Black family had not been destroyed.

Regulating Civil Disorder

The regulatory functions of the modern welfare state were ushered in with the Social Security Act of 1935 under the threat of a crumbling economy and as a result of shifts in family formation. High unemployment rates at the time led those without jobs to agitate for assistance with mass protests taking place in Chicago and Kansas City among other cities (Piven and Cloward 1993). In response welfare programs were inaugurated to "mute civil disorder." This was a tactic that had been used since the sixteenth century in western societies including France, Germany, and England (Piven and Cloward 1993: xv). More recently welfare policy was used in response to disorder at the height of the civil and welfare rights movement in the 1960s.

Beginning in the 1960s a series of social and economic upheavals that specifically affected Blacks increased their vulnerability to poverty (Amott 1990). Black migration from the South to the North, based on the erroneous belief that employment would be accessible, resulted in a concentration of Blacks in urban areas (Patterson 1994; Jones 1992). The combination of population density, economic dislocation, and political disenfranchisement led to unrest in urban Black communities, which came to a head and resulted in demands for civil rights.[3] As Handler (1995) notes, "along with civil rights there was a legal rights revolution. The federal courts and welfare rights activists forced open the ADC gates" (28), and in 1962 ADC was transformed into a program Aid to Families with Dependent Children (AFDC). At the same time, the Democratic Party worked to placate urban Blacks, as they tried to secure the Black vote. In fact Skocpol (1988) argues that the War on Poverty in the 1960s, which included increased access to public assistance, was the result of Black demands on the Democratic Party, as more Blacks migrated to urban areas. This can be seen as another example of the use of welfare to regulate discontent.

The success of grassroots organizing and of the civil rights movement brought some respite from previous rigid eligibility rules, altering welfare's historic unresponsiveness to Black women. These shifts came in response to the rapid rise in the number of Black families headed by females (Brewer 1988) combined with Black women's participation in the welfare rights movement, through which they were encouraged to lobby for their right to income support (Piven and Cloward 1979; West 1981). Through the National Welfare Rights Organization, women demanded that the state ease restrictions on eligibility rules (Abramovitz 1996).

Consequently, the number of Black women receiving aid expanded, blurring the original criteria used to distinguish those deserving of assistance from others; that is, Whiteness and being widowed. Ultimately, Black women's use of welfare brought forth "a crisis," according to Walters (1999), resulting in the implementation of new restrictive policies that undermined Black women's entitlement to assistance. Furthermore, as they came to be overrepresented on the AFDC rolls, relative to their percentage of the population, negative images of Black women proliferated serving to de-legitimize them as recipients. Ideology produces meanings, as Mullings (1994) states, "which are generated, maintained and deployed in relation to the distribution of power. Dominant ideology sets out a framework by which hierarchy is explained" (266). The popular construction of Black women on welfare was rooted in a raced sexual-political ideology[4] and cemented the negative association between Black women and welfare, drawing on stereotypes that circulated among the public.

Imagining Black Women on Welfare

Images perpetuated by the media, politicians, and scholars strengthen misconceptions about women and welfare. One result has been that Black women on welfare are offered up as " . . . the agent of destruction, the creator of the pathological Black urban poor family from which all ills flow; a monster creating crack dealers, addicts, muggers and rapists—men who become those things because of being immersed in her culture of poverty" (Lubiano 1992: 339). Black women, then, are seen as unworthy users of welfare—they are considered to be chiselers, brood mares, and lazy matriarchs (Mink 1998; Roberts 1997; Jewell 1993). Meanwhile there are little if any negative images of women of other racial and ethnic groups, particularly White women receiving assistance, circulating in the public sphere. But depictions of Black women on welfare are seared into the minds of the public, and it is they who are charged with multiple transgressions, moral and otherwise, wreaking havoc with the intentions of a welfare state that was meant to help the "deserving poor."

Differentiation spawned stereotypes that one could easily connect to the stringent rules imposed especially against Black single mothers, in order to make them ineligible for assistance. One example was the "man in the house" rule. "Man in the house" rules translated into the denial of benefits for children, if the mother associated with a man in a relationship that was similar to that of a husband and wife. These rules frequently meant Black women were unable to access assistance (Bell 1965). But regardless, Black single mothers received assistance, raising the angst and ire of conservatives. Regulating the Black family took on a new twist, in part based on Moynihan's report (1965), which blamed single Black mothers for many of the upheavals of the 1960s, including poverty, riots, and protests. According to Quadagno (1994), the National Advisory Commission on Civil Disorders determined that Black male unemployment contributed to problems in urban areas, but the logic of the theory was linked to Black women's work, just as it had been in 1935. Their productive labor was an enigma, a challenge to the Black family structure and Black male privilege.

Black women bore the burden of responsibility for social ills, including riots. It was believed that children growing up under the condition of female-headed households were "likely participants in civil disorder" (Quadagno 1994: 125). It is now well known that the governmental solution to the urban turmoil "caused" by Black women's working was to provide incentives to lure "Black males to become family breadwinners

and for Black women to stay home with their children"
(Quadagno 1994: 125). One solution came in the form of the
Family Assistance Program (FAP), proposed by President
Nixon, a work incentive program to get men working, which
would supposedly interrupt Black children's tendencies
towards delinquency. The plan would have cut social welfare
but would have guaranteed a family of four with an annual
income of $2,600. In other words, the FAP was going to help
stifle rioting (by offering money), placate the public (by cutting
social welfare), and build a Republican base of supporters
(those who did not support the provision of welfare). The
plan, however, died in the Senate in 1972, the same year
Nixon said "workfare not welfare," which emphasized not a
federal guarantee of funding, but rather a focus on driving the
poor and the working poor toward participation in the low-
wage labor market (Prashad 2003). This approach differs sig-
nificantly from the Keynesian welfare state and represents a
neoliberal approach in which profit, free market initiatives,
contraction of public spending, and privatization of public
programs and resources, prevail (Lyon-Callo 2004).

Work-related programs were inaugurated as the backbone
of welfare policy-making, which then, as now, is ironic because
poverty among Blacks worsened during the inception of these
work-based programs between the 1970s and the 1980s.
According to Quadagno, during the 1970s Black unemployment was at 13.6% (just about twice that of White unemployment), the percent of children born into a single-parent family
was 62.6%, and inner cities were in decline. Conservatives
maintained that these conditions were caused by the welfare
state. Presently work-based welfare is mandatory in an economic climate where Blacks are nearly twice as likely to be
unemployed as Whites.[5]

Beginning in the 1980s a feverish pitch charged that welfare "dependency" was to blame for social ills and high rates
of taxation (Solinger 1999). Conservatives embraced arguments put forth by right-wing scholars, which suggested that
crime, unemployment, and single parenthood were *caused* by
welfare use as opposed to structural deficits (Gilder 1981).

Mead (1986b), for example, argued that the welfare system created dependency because recipients are able to collect benefits without any responsibility to "give back." These observations may be viewed as attacks on government intervention as a strategy for addressing poverty, which is characteristic of neoliberalism—that is, minimizing government intervention; intensifying and expanding market strategies based on principles of competition by increasing the number, frequency, repeatability, and formalization of transactions. Neoliberalism rests on privatization, corporatization, marketplace participation and consumption of services. Thus, a neoliberal strategy argues that social problems like poverty are best addressed by pushing people into wage labor and forcing them to be consumers of services; i.e. "buying" their assistance. Although not only a product of neoliberalism, the assumption was, if programs like AFDC did not exist, then poor people would be forced to become "attached to employment" increasing the feasibility of the two-parent family. Public sentiment supported changes in welfare fueled by conservative arguments that welfare encouraged Black women to avoid marriage and bear more children in order to receive increased benefits (Gilder 1987). Of course much of what has driven elites' welfare policy agenda has been the need to control Black women's sexuality by drumming up charges of their immorality. Several forms of reproductive control aimed at Black women have wormed their way into welfare policy. But, even prior to welfare reform, there were precedents for reproductive control, justified on the grounds that Black women were allegedly hyperfertile. Thus welfare reform may also be viewed as a mechanism to regulate Black women's fertility.

Reproduction and Welfare

Although there is a long history of asserting control over all women's reproductive capacities (Petchesky 1995) particular attention has been directed toward the reproductive capacity of women of color (see for example, Rodrique 1990; Lopez 1987).

Growing concern about women giving birth out of wedlock gave way to yet another regulatory component of welfare—that is, the use of sanctions to try and discourage Black women (and other women of color) from having children.

In Dorothy Roberts's *Killing the Black Body* (1997), the point is made that one goal of welfare is to reduce the number of children born to women receiving public assistance. Policies aimed at this goal have taken a number of forms including the use of the Family Cap Law, a birth-deterring provision. Roberts notes that "under the family cap, a family's standard of need is not adjusted upward to accommodate the new child. These laws are premised on the assumption that the promise of benefits entices women to have additional children" (210).[6]

Regulating reproduction through welfare includes incentives based on birth control targeted at women, specifically Norplant, a synthetic hormone released in low dosages, which suppresses ovulation and prevents pregnancy for up to 5 years. The FDA approved Norplant in 1990, which was immediately viewed as a way to control the "underclass," a pejorative term frequently associated with poor Blacks (Kimmelman 1990 cited in Roberts 1997).

Restrictions on Black women's reproductive capacity have been connected to welfare primarily because, although Black women comprise 6% of the U.S. population, they represent one-third of AFDC recipients. With many Black welfare recipients living in inner cities, it is no accident that Norplant has been dispensed in these communities (Roberts 1997). Campaigns to distribute Norplant have targeted teens living in Baltimore, Los Angeles, and Chicago. Roberts reports that politicians in other states such as Kansas, Connecticut, Louisiana, Arizona, Colorado, Ohio, Florida, and Washington have offered financial incentives to welfare recipients if they agree to use Norplant. The most coercive form of reproductive regulation through welfare with regard to Norplant were bills introduced in the states of Maryland, Mississippi, and South Carolina, which would have required that all recipients of welfare be mandated to get Norplant inserted as a condition of eligibility for welfare benefits.

⟨❧⟩

My goal has been to point out the regulatory functions of welfare policy across several domains: the management of civil disorder, productive labor, domestic labor, family formation, images, and reproduction. Embedded in each we find gender- and race-specific forms of domination with policies informing programs and practices that maintain hierarchical arrangements and continue to support middle-class and White privilege. One question is: How are the historically constituted regulatory practices of welfare articulated in contemporary welfare reform policy?

Welfare Reform

On August 22, 1996, President William Jefferson Clinton signed the Personal Responsibility and Work Opportunity Reconciliation Act (PRWORA). The Act replaced the AFDC program that had existed since the 1960s for women and children and replaced it with a program known as Temporary Assistance for Needy Families (TANF). The Act also replaced Home Relief for Single Adults, Jobs Opportunities and Basic Skill Training Program (JOBS), and emergency assistance with the Safety Net Program, a state-funded program for single adults. The most well-known components of the law are the 5-year lifetime maximums for receipt of cash benefits and the mandatory work requirements.

President Clinton did not initiate the changes in welfare; rather, he completed a process of ideological convergence between decreasing liberal support of welfare policy and increasing conservative sentiment regarding the distorted moral impropriety of government assistance. Prior to the 1980s, liberals generally considered welfare to be an entitlement that upheld the right of AFDC mothers to not work, although typically they *did* work sometimes in unregulated markets such as child care workers (Handler 1995), while conservatives have considered AFDC to be a problem since 1967. AFDC has been viewed as a crisis by successive presidents and Congress, and many administrations have tried to pass or have successfully passed legislation that required recipients to work through incentive programs. The enactment of the Work Incentive Program (WIN) in 1967 illustrates this point. The WIN program made receipt of welfare contingent upon work; adult participants and children over age 16 had to be employed to ensure assistance. If a recipient did not participate, her grant was reduced. In 1971 Congress enacted WIN II, in which mothers with children over age 6 had to participate in employment, with direct job placement emphasized over education and training.

Following the WIN program was the Family Support Act of 1988 (FSA), which had liberal support and focused on providing education and training to move people from AFDC to work by guaranteeing child care and work-search related assistance. JOBS, a program of FSA, promoted job search and job readiness activities. It was the Family Support Act that signaled the first shift in liberals' previous acknowledgment that women on welfare should not have to work. This ideological shift emerged alongside women's increased participation in the paid labor force, which proved that if nonwelfare women with children could work, women on welfare could also work. It also emerged in tandem with changes that sought to reduce barriers to "economic growth." Thus the centerpiece of the 1996 welfare reform was the mandate that recipients work or engage in work-related programs as a way to reduce dependency on welfare and decrease the rolls.

Temporary Assistance to Needy Families (TANF) is a block grant from the federal government, which provides states with an annual Family Assistance Grant. The Family Assistance Grant may only be used to assist households with children or pregnant women. In addition to the 5-year lifetime limit on the receipt of federal funds and the requirement that recipients must work or be engaged in a work-related activity, another aspect of the law is that TANF funding may be denied to pregnant teens under the age of 18.

States were given considerable discretion in designing their work programs and a great deal of flexibility to determine the mix of services they would provide. In New York, for example, work and immediate attachment to work-related activities became the tenets of the State's new program, and educational and training programs are only made available to clients to the extent that they can be counted toward meeting the federally mandated participation rates for the percentage of people who must be in work-related activities. A recipient must be involved in a work experience program 20 to 35 hours per week within 2 months of initial receipt of aid. Mothers with infants as young as 3 months are required to work outside the home, unless they are unable to secure childcare. These policies were critiqued by advocates, including battered women's advocates, who argued that violence was indeed a barrier to welfare reform's goals of putting people to work.

Poverty and Violence: The Connection to Welfare Reform

Violence against women is an epidemic that can be measured by data showing that between 1992 and 1996, approximately 8 out of every 1,000 women age 12 or older experienced victimization (Greenfield, et al., 1998). Violence and poverty raise concerns because leaving abusive situations is often hampered by economic deprivation (Kenney and Brown 1996; Martin 1976; Okun 1986). In making connections between the social problems of poverty and violence, researchers have shown that significant percentages of women on welfare report physical abuse, as they did for example, in Worcester, Massachusetts. There, a five-year study of homeless and poorly housed mothers, the majority of whom were on AFDC, found that 32% of the women were currently in battering relationships (Bassuk, et al., 1996).

Recent research on poor women shows they are more likely to experience violence than women with higher household incomes. Rates of women's victimization by an intimate was 21.3 per 1,000 in households with less than $7,500, while women with household incomes of $7,500 to $14,999 were 12.3 per 1,000 (United States Department of Justice 1998). More recently it has been shown that women living in households with lower annual incomes experience violence seven times greater than women living in households with the highest annual household income, 20 per 1,000 versus 3 per 1,000 (Rennison and Welchans 2000).

Several explanations have been proposed to understand the higher rate of violence among the poor. One is that men in low-income groups legitimize violence more than other men, as they hold more traditional gender ideologies (Collins 1988). A second reason suggested is that lower income men have fewer ways of controlling women than other men. In other words, men with higher incomes can more easily control women by restricting their access to economic resources, whereas men with lower incomes may resort to violence (Kurz 1999). An elaboration on the last point suggests that poor men's inability to provide for their family exacerbates shame, which is then transformed into violence (Gilligan 1996). Raphael (2000) adds that women's economic potential, in relation to men's lack of economic potential, might trigger male violence. A final explanation may be that poor people are more likely to be subjected to institutional surveillance and interventions, which could account for higher rates of reporting violence in the first place.

Critics of welfare reform, mostly advocates in the battered women's movement, argued that the hardship of violence might prevent women from complying with their state's work requirements (see for example Raphael 1999; Brandwein 1999; Kurz 1999; Polakow 1999a), pushing families deeper into poverty. If unable to meet work requirements, women would lose their welfare benefits, forcing them to stay with their abusers. Furthermore, the long-term effects of abuse may create a *continuing need for welfare*. In response to these concerns a flexible policy option was proposed that would help women to disengage or separate from violent situations.

Senators Paul Wellstone (Democrat, Minnesota) and Patti Murray (Democrat, Washington) crafted and sponsored the

Family Violence Amendment to the Federal Personal Responsibility Act. The Family Violence Option (FVO [Sec. 402(a)
(7)]), permits states to: 1) screen for domestic violence both for
candidates applying for assistance and for those being dropped
from assistance programs; 2) refer victims of domestic violence
to counseling; and 3) make a determination whether certain
welfare requirements should be waived for abused women,
such as time limits, having to apply for child support, and
work requirements that would unfairly penalize women for
mandates they may not be able to meet while in or leaving an
abusive relationship (Kurz 1999: 143).

Approximately 41 states have implemented the FVO with
conflicting opinions about its success. Some domestic violence
advocates felt that women who disclosed the violence in their
lives would be dealt with punitively by caseworkers and/or
that abusive partners would be retaliatory. Others felt that the
Option would lead to the view that battered women were
unable to work, and still others felt that there would be
uneven access to and uneven distribution of the waivers, based
on race and class.

Constricting Freedom

Beyond battered women's advocates, scholars have argued that
welfare reform has "disabled almost every aspect of women's
citizenship" (Mink 1999: 6). Some charge that welfare reform
was built around a growing process of pathologizing women,
poor and Black women in particular (Solinger 1999). For
example, Mead ideologically annihilates welfare recipients
saying they are "semi-socialized" and "They are remarkably
unresponsive to economic incentives . . . [the purpose of policy
is] not to expand the freedom of . . . recipients. It is, in fact, to
constrict their freedom [emphasis mine] in necessary ways"
(Mead 1986b, cited in Solinger 1999: 16).

Although many speak of welfare reform as if it were a new
policy, various aspects of it have been in rehearsal since 1935,
when programs were especially malevolent toward Blacks, who

were systematically denied benefits. In the 1960s, when Black women began to challenge their exclusion from receiving benefits, new tools of regulation emerged, such as midnight raids to catch men living with women, in which case eligibility could be revoked. Then, in the 1990s, Black women were again regulated through welfare policy, and this ethnography examines how welfare reform practices conspire to control Black women, specifically those who are battered. Both single women and women with children encounter rules that undermine equal access in context of economic restructuring, placing them at risk for deeper poverty, and render almost meaningless PRWORA's stated goal of creating "self-sufficiency."

Oh Sister, Shelter Me

In many ways this is a multisited ethnography, taking place in Angel House Shelter, the city of Laneville, and the River Valley Department of Social Services. Sometimes each of these entities felt like separate spheres with their own logic of control. For example, Angel House has rules and regulations that organize the process of sheltering. Angel House is located in the city of Laneville, which was a casualty of global economics. Laneville's precarious economy controlled women's housing options and limited their work opportunities. Finally, the River Valley County Department of Social Services is the institution that regulates poor and working-class people in the counties' municipalities through the implementation of welfare policy. But sometimes these entities congealed into a web in which women were caught, with no clear path out.

Women operate simultaneously in all three spheres primarily because by state law they are only permitted to live in a shelter for 90 days, and they must immediately apply or reapply for social services upon their arrival to pay for their shelter stay and to facilitate securing a permanent residence. Within 24 to 48 hours of arriving at Angel House, they are literally living at the intersection of a shelter, the city, and social services trying to establish independent lives. In order to understand the spaces the women in this ethnography entered, this chapter provides a window into the histories of the city of Laneville and Angel House. The order in which they are described reflects my entrée, not necessarily the women's, some of whom came to the shelter in Laneville from different cities and states. Others already lived in Laneville or its surrounding areas and then came to the shelter after experiencing abuse. A separate discussion of the River Valley Department of Social Services is found in chapter 4, as it is a distinct analytic theme.

Laneville, New York

Laneville is located in River Valley County, part of the Upstate Region of New York, and the county is home to nearly 260,000 of whom 88% are White. The county reports a median family income of $49,000 and a per capita income of nearly $26,000. In terms of employment, 13% of the private sector jobs in this part of New York are located in River Valley with a high percentage of professional and technical workers living in the county. Many districts comprise River Valley, but it is Laneville that has the largest Black and Latino population of all the districts in the county.

At the turn of the twentieth century Laneville had a population of 26,000. While the population increased to 41,000 by 1950, as of the 1990 census only about 4,000 more people live in Laneville than in 1900. With just about 30,000 residents, approximately 32% are Black. Laneville also has pockets of poverty, and of the nearly 12,000 households, 52% fall into the low-, very low- and extremely low-income categories. According to the U. S. Department of Housing and Urban Development, 38% of the households earned less than $17,499. In April 2000 Laneville's unemployment rate was 4.9%, almost four times that of the closet town (Resident Civilian Labor Force Summary n.d.). For those who are working, major employers include the City of Laneville, a local hospital, the gas and electric company, the City of Laneville school district, and the largest private employer Zytron Corporation. Shelter staff, volunteers, and community residents told me their family members presently work or have worked for this particular company, and several shelter residents told me they wanted to work there.

The juxtaposition of history and modernity are evident, as the train approaches the Laneville station. The first thing one notices is a large, abandoned brick building with paint that has aged over time. On the building one can just make out letters spelling the name of a company, but what one can clearly read is the portion of the sign that reads: "Founded in 1858." This building is one of many structural remnants of the area's manufacturing history, which throughout the nineteenth century, along with the shipping trades, dominated Laneville's economy. Textile mills thrived, and later on when the railroad was built, the area became a "playground" for wealthy New Yorkers who donated money for the development of major institutions in the county. As such, Laneville and the county in which it is located are replete with libraries, historical societies, and institutions of higher learning, as well as being home to a number of national and state historic sites.

From the moment one exits the train and enters the station, the city's historic grandeur is apparent beginning with the architecturally impressive train station. Walking away from the station, the views are spectacular, as are the old brick, wood, and stone residences and commercial buildings, erected in the late nineteenth and early twentieth centuries.

Laneville's city center illustrates the irony of its history and manifestations of contemporary "urban" life. Historic pubs are across from public housing. Or, a palatial former mansion, currently a cultural center that promotes local artists, sits opposite residential buildings in front of which drug deals take place throughout the day and night as does small-scale prostitution. Along the commercial strip many businesses have closed since the late 1970s, evidenced by the number of unoccupied storefronts. In 1988 a design firm performed a façade study of the commercial area and found out that of 160 buildings surveyed, 18 had vacant first floors. My own self-guided neighborhood mapping of this commercial strip found 26 buildings boarded up or empty with "For Rent" signs posted in the windows, including the Haupsberg Building, which was Laneville's main department store in the late 1860s. The 100,000-square-foot building closed in the early 1980s and now, near where the vacant Haupsberg is located, are hair shops, music stores, insurance companies, check-cashing businesses, and stores with partially empty shelves. Interspersed among these service economy establishments are empty storefronts with faded signage.

Sheltering Battered Women

Prior to the 1970s, the United States had no governmental policy to address the housing, welfare, and employment needs of battered women (Dobash and Dobash 1992). The battered women's movement grew out of the organizing efforts of local groups and individuals that coalesced into a social movement in the 1970s. Members of the movement exposed the severity of violence against women and challenged the invisibility of women's abuse. One major outcome of the battered women's movement was increased public awareness of domestic violence and the positioning of battering as a social problem (Kanuha 1996; Loseke 1992), and by 1982 legislative efforts to protect women and support shelters existed in every state in the country.[1] By 1990 there were 1,500 shelters for battered women in the country.

Shelters have two primary goals. First, they offer a secure escape from violence, and second, they serve as a "stepping stone to independence" (Loseke 1992: 32). Shelter staff make referrals, offer individual and group support, and engage in advocacy to help women negotiate bureaucracies and assist them in recreating their lives. Since battered women's needs go beyond safety, shelter staff provide assistance in accessing places to live, identifying strategies to alleviate poverty, securing legal protections, and advocating for battered women's rights with human service agencies. Assistance in these areas facilitates women's ability to leave and remain free of abusive relationships in order to begin anew. These advocacy efforts are necessary because historically, women's experiences with human service agencies have been humiliating (Martin 1976). Feminist researchers have found that some caseworkers at welfare agencies do not support battered women, and there is often a disparity between women's assessments of their abuse and the caseworkers' own evaluation—that the problem is not that serious. Thus, shelters offer more than safe space; they are also an alternative to the offensiveness of traditional human services (Hoff 1990).

Another outcome of the battered women's movement was the utilization of welfare to assist women in extricating themselves from violence. In New York the strategy of funding domestic violence shelters through the department of social services was instituted in 1978.[2] The scheme was, and continues to be, unique in the United States because shelters in almost every other state receive funding through block grants. In New York, shelter funding comes from the New York State Department of Social Services, which administers payment for housing and cash benefits through reimbursement.

Over 1.5 million women are victimized annually, indicating the need for shelters (Tjaden and Thoennes 1998: 2 and 5). In New York State in 1995, 4,848 battered women and 6,591 children received residential services from domestic violence programs, and a total of 23,164 persons were denied shelter in 1995, primarily due to lack of available space (New York State Department of Social Services 1995a). If women and their children in New York need a place to go and room is available, they may go to 1 of 91 approved residential services, including Angel House (New York State Department of Social Services 1995a).

Angel House

In 1977 a group of women from River Valley County formed a task force that identified the need for domestic violence services. The group planned to initiate a hotline and create housing for battered women. Around the same time in 1978, the Board of Deacons of the Laneville Presbyterian Church developed a response to meet the needs of battered women and children. After several years of trying to secure funding for a shelter, both groups collaborated and decided to use the Church's parsonage as the first shelter space, because it was no longer in use. The group named the shelter Angel House after a former church member, Mary Angel who was an active member of the church and whose family's trust originally funded the parsonage. Angel House formally opened its doors in 1981, coinciding with the new state law permitting women leaving their spouses due to domestic violence to receive assistance from the Department of Social Services. According to Jean Ann Richardson, the shelter's first executive director: "It was a four-bedroom house with four beds in each room and 1 small room with two beds. We were able to negotiate housing for 17 people. There was no privacy and it was very difficult."

Over time space limitations and increasing need necessitated the search for a new building. Subsequently, Angel House relocated from the church to a residential block in Laneville. The new shelter is in an old house to which an addition was built to accommodate more women and children. The original house is where most of the staff offices are located. On the first floor of the original house are the kitchen and a large dining room, where the staff spend their time when not counseling women. The former living room in the old house is now office space for the child advocate and the housing specialist. The second floor has one bathroom and three offices, one each for the finance director, the information systems manager, and the shelter director.

Women and children live in the new addition, which was designed to correct the deficits of the previous shelter, where there was neither enough play space for children, nor private space for women. On the first floor there is a children's playroom as well as a child therapy room with a door leading to a spacious backyard. There are three bedrooms, one full bath that is wheelchair accessible, and a half bath. Women have access to a laundry room, smoking room, and an adult recreation room, which is off limits to children. The kitchen is large with cabinets for each woman to keep her own food, if she wants to buy special items not provided by the shelter. Adjacent to the kitchen is a large dining room for communal meals, often decorated with crafts and posters made by residents and children who participate in the arts and crafts program. The living room looks out onto the backyard and is furnished with sturdy "This-End-Up"-type furniture that can withstand romping children. The second floor also has a laundry facility, five bedrooms, and two bathrooms as well as the house manager's office.

The increasing number of battered women, combined with a shortage of housing for women leaving the shelter, precipitated Angel House to open a second shelter in 1996 further up county and to operate a Section 8 subsidized apartment complex in Laneville. The organization has an annual budget of $1 million dollars with 60% of the income coming from reimbursements through the Department of Social Services. An additional $126,000 comes from the Section 8 rental income. Remaining funds are raised through federal and state grants, the United Way, and individual contributions.

Making the decision to come to the shelter is full of mixed emotions, and women contend with many issues, particularly if they have children. The potential of danger, however, requires that women make decisions quickly, although they do so with a lot of trepidation. Below is a field note excerpt on shelter life 2 months after I started volunteering.

April 1998—A Day in the Life of a Shelter
I arrived at the shelter at 8:45 a.m. Margaret, Anne, and Lucy were in a jovial mood. They sat at the large dining room table on the staff side of the building eating breakfast. We talked about the weather, and where the Laneville Journal was (the women need the paper to find jobs and apartments). The phone rang, and Margaret picked up. She thought I should respond and take on my first hotline call. On the line was Trudi a woman from Ghana.

Trudi said she wanted to leave her husband because he allowed their adopted daughter to hit her. We stayed on the phone for 30 to 40 minutes, while she decided whether she wanted to come to the shelter. She could not decide how she felt about leaving her house. She did not want to disrupt her biological daughter's life, nor did she think she should have to be the one to go. Trudi came from Ghana two-and-a-half years ago with her birth daughter Jane who is 10, her husband Sam, and an informally adopted daughter, Mari who is now 17. Sam has turned Mari into a cowife. He encourages her to hit Trudi, knowing enough about U.S. values and law to not hit Trudi himself. But he also beats Jane with sticks. Recently, Mari slapped Trudi and bit her fingers, drawing blood. Trudi was frightened and called Sam to tell him she was bleeding and requested that he drive her to the hospital. She placed the call at 4:30 p.m., but he did not come home until 10:00 p.m. When Sam arrived, Trudi asked to be taken to the hospital. He told Mari to lock the car door and not let Trudi in. After much begging, he permitted Trudi to get in the car. Instead of driving her to the hospital, he dropped her off at the police station. She was crying uncontrollably. It appears that Sam's plan was to have the police see her in an agitated state, so there would be a witness to her "irrational" behavior.

Trudi was hesitant about coming to the shelter because she feared that while filling out paperwork, Sam would go to school and pick up Jane. She wanted to make sure that if she left him, she would have custody of Jane. At first, Trudi wanted us to hold a bed for her until 4:00 p.m., but I told her that the shelter would have to give a bed to whomever called. There are only 20 beds for women and children. We were nearing 16 today and at that rate of occupancy, beds get filled very quickly.

Trudi agreed to be picked up at the River Valley County Department of Social Services (RVCDSS) at 11:45 a.m. Margaret and I drove together to pick her up . . . As we left, she cried the whole ride back to the shelter. I returned to the shelter and sat in the front counseling office. I then did my first intake. Trudi signed permission and release forms, I copied her Medicaid card and driver's license. I placed all the materials in her case file. Every resident has a file with intake information, including all the community and case management contacts made by and on behalf of a resident.

Phones were ringing off the hook today. Kids running in and out of the playroom. Lots of noise. In between these distractions, I informed Trudi about the mandatory house meetings on Thursday nights and the group meetings on Friday at 10:30 a.m. Also, she would have to follow curfew rules and sign out when she left the building. Trudi told me she was so happy to be at the shelter. All she wanted at that moment was to sleep and "get things together."

While I completed the intake, Margaret called the court to explore the next steps for Trudi to get an order of protection (OOP) and temporary custody of Jane. She also called Jane's school to arrange for her to be picked up before her father arrived. We finished the paperwork, then left to pick up Jane from school.

When we arrived, the headmaster, Mr. Alonzo, invited us to sit in the lunchroom so we could discuss why Jane was being picked up. As Trudi spoke, tears streamed from her eyes. Mr. Alonzo challenged Trudi, saying that nothing could possibly be wrong because her husband was such a nice man. Besides, he said, Jane never told anyone at school that there were problems in the house. When Trudi told him she was leaving her husband because he beat her, Mr. Alonzo responded, "Well you can't just leave him."

We went back to the shelter. I took Trudi on a tour and helped her get settled in her room. From the supply closet we got sheets, towels, and toiletries . . . we continued with the tour. I informed Trudi that all residents take turns making dinner for everybody in the house. She wondered aloud if they might eat a traditional dish from Ghana.

While Trudi and Jane got settled, Margaret was on the phone getting information about ensuring Trudi's custody of Jane. She found out that Trudi had 15 minutes to make it down to the courthouse to file a complaint and request custody for the judge to hear her case tomorrow. We jumped in the van, drove to River Valley County Courthouse. Margaret dropped us off and we entered the building. As we were standing at the sign-in desk, Trudi and I both felt someone behind us. When we turned around, Trudi looked petrified. "That's my husband," she whispered, "I had a feeling he was following us all day." Sam just stood there quietly looking at us with his hands in his pockets. I thought he might have a gun or knife, but all he wanted was for Jane to come to him. He asked me if he could take his daughter. I summoned up enough courage and firmly said, "No!" Just at that moment a legal advocate came out, assessed the situation, and quickly took us into her office. Margaret came back to court to relieve me. When I met Margaret in the waiting area, we discovered that Trudi's husband was simultaneously filing for custody. Sam's presence meant that I had to have an escort sneak me out of the building in case he followed me. (He didn't, but I was still anxious).

During their first 24 hours at the shelter, residents must complete an application for public assistance, which hopefully will cover the cost of staying at the shelter. The application is dropped off at RVCDSS for the woman by a staff person, intern, or volunteer. Supposedly, this reduces the amount of waiting time for her first interview. Even if she has public assistance, her budget has to be modified to ensure that a housing allowance is paid to the shelter. If she does not apply for public assistance or is turned down by RVCDSS, she may be asked to pay some portion of the cost of her stay at the shelter, as little as $5 a day.

Women are expected to fully participate in shelter life, including going to group and individual meetings. Some meetings serve to educate women about the dynamics of abuse and to reduce feelings of isolation. Residents must attend all group meetings during their first two weeks at the shelter, after which some are optional. But two weekly meetings are never optional: the mandatory Thursday night meetings and the Friday morning meetings. Thursday night meetings are facilitated by the house manager. She democratically allocates cooking and cleaning chores among residents. Friday morning meetings are facilitated by any one of the advocates to develop cohesion among residents, discuss community issues, such as how gossip is hurtful, and to reinforce the rules of shelter life.

If she has children, the woman will meet with a child advocate and perhaps the child specialist. Typically, each woman has an assigned caseworker, although her case may be handled by any one of 10 staff or student interns. From the moment they settle in, someone is assigned to help the women through the process of becoming housed. Women's lives at the shelter are focused on leaving, since residents are only permitted to stay for 90 days, (although she may return at a later date, if necessary).

Residents must live by shelter rules, such as abiding by the curfew. If the rules are broken, women may be asked to leave. For example, in November 1998, one resident, Georgina, stayed out past curfew twice. Each time she stayed out, she said it was because she had to work overnight at the Stop 'N Shop. During staff meeting, a caseworker pointed out that this particular Stop 'N Shop is not open 24 hours. By the third time Georgina broke curfew, there was a lengthy back-and-forth around the dining room table as to whether or not Georgina really wanted to be asked to leave, since she continued to break curfew. Staff wanted to know what she was doing. Was she testing their trust? Several days later, Georgina broke curfew a fourth time and was asked to leave the shelter, but it was an agonizing decision.

Staff struggle with how much flexibility to give women who break curfew and other rules. They recognize that shelter life rules sometimes counter how women envision this period of reprieve from the violence in their lives. At the same time when women directly refuse to follow the rules or are confrontational, staff will "diagnose" women's behavior as being "noncompliant," which Georgina, was considered to be.

Staff responsibilities include being on call on a rotational basis. Each advocate works diligently with women to develop achievable goals in preparation for her departure. Each day brings its own drama, and what may appear to be an easily resolvable problem can turn into a monumental project. In May of 1998, a White woman, Traci, came to the shelter from a hospital, which had neglected to give her an important prescription. Traci had no insurance to cover the cost of medication, yet it was essential for her recovery. Occasionally advocates work with agencies like Catholic Charities to assist women in need. In this case, Traci's physician was nowhere to be found, and a hard copy of the "scrip" or prescription was needed in order for Catholic Charities to process the emergency payment request. Contact was made with the doctor's secretary, who checked the validity of the prescription. Then the "scrip" was called in to the only pharmacy in Laneville that accepts payment from Catholic Charities instead of the consumer.

All went smoothly, until Catholic Charities demanded an original copy of the prescription. This was impossible to obtain because the doctor could not be located and was therefore unable to provide a physical copy. It took four hours to get the prescription filled.

Daily summaries of each day's events are logged in the "shift change" book. Shift change is a journal that captures the daily goings-on at the shelter. For example, the four-hour process of obtaining medication for Traci was reduced to a three-line description in shift change. It describes tensions between shelter residents as well as those between the women and staff; there are updates on who has come and gone; and other concerns, such as those about children's behavior, are all logged in shift change. Shift change also chronicles moments when absolutely nothing has occurred (which are rare), and when creative resolutions to problems have been generated. For example one entry referred to putting dinner plates in all the windows of the shelter because one resident thought her batterer had found out where she was living. The plates served as an extra sensitive security system; if any window was opened, the plates would fall down and everyone in the house would know to call the police immediately.

Angel House is a haven of safety, as described by Trudi, and a place of imposed order, as seen through Georgina's experience. From these paradoxical points Angel House is still the place from where women begin to rebuild their lives, usually in Laneville. Against the backdrop of shelter life, women also encounter various forms of management, as they become engaged with the reformed welfare system.

4

Ceremonies of Degradation

Battered women's experiences with control do not end when they leave their batterer but continue after they have left those violent situations to set up households apart from their batterers. While some recognize the role of welfare as a way for battered women to secure economic and social independence (Davis 1999), the fact of the matter is that welfare produces its own form of institutional regulation. Obtaining basic everyday needs for those who are poor or low income includes a series of micro-steps involving interactions with multiple institutions. When a woman is poor, battered, and in a shelter, a number of bureaucratic relationships are initiated for her to accomplish each task of ensuring that basic needs are met and safety guaranteed. She may need social services to find an apartment, have the utilities turned on, obtain health care, find child care, and purchase food. The River Valley Department of Social Services (RVCDSS) was one of the most significant institutional environments in which women interacted and within this complex setting, power over women's lives was exerted.

This chapter examines the practices used to investigate women for the purposes of determining their eligibility for services. It underscores how women who need welfare are viewed as fraudulent and shows the rituals deployed to divert women from continuing the application process. Welfare offices in the United States have a long history of client maltreatment, and workers within the system have employed tactics to regulate and control the welfare population such as the "man in the house" rules and midnight raids of the 1960s. But out of welfare reform policy new deterrent strategies have been manufactured, making it difficult to access services and resources. Essentially permission has been extended to caseworkers to discourage people from applying for or continuing to receive assistance. In order to receive whatever meager resources they can secure, women are subjected to various degrees of humiliation and degradation in their interactions with institutional personnel.

First, the physical environment of the Department of Social Services is not a welcoming place to those walking through the doors: one immediately senses that they are trespassers, a feeling brought on by the presence of security guards and sometimes police officers. Then, interactions with frontline workers are often demeaning. Finally, caseworkers' off-putting attitudes can dissuade women from pursuing TANF or Safety Net funding.

For Black women, some of these interactions are burdened by preexisting notions about their welfare use that lace the public's and social service workers' ideas about dependency and deceit. The racial politics of welfare has long constructed the client/subject in negative terms, a residual outcome of racial anxiety based on the belief that Black women have lots of children, are too dependent upon the government, and are welfare cheats (Gilens 1999; Lubiano 1992). These distortions, of course, were formalized in a naming ceremony, when 1976 presidential candidate Ronald Reagan offered the public an image of women on welfare who were living well and driving expensive cars all at the expense of the "honest" taxpayer, naming them "Welfare Queens" (Zucchino 1999).

Many of the women with whom I spoke believe that social service caseworkers are predisposed against poor Black women, and caseworkers' presumptions managed to bleed into caseworker/client interactions. Assumptions were never directly stated, but innocuous insults such as looks and tone of voice led women to conclude that racism was very much a part of welfare. Some, like Michelle and Elizabeth talked about how they thought social service caseworkers viewed them in terms of popular images: as long-term welfare users and as unmotivated enough to change their lives. Generally women were on the defensive even before meeting caseworkers and often came to expect only the worst. The increase in deterrent strategies exacerbated women's cynicism, and sometimes they simply left the social service office, too discouraged to pursue the process any further.

Going to Social Services

On a sunny afternoon I walked from the shelter to the River Valley County Department of Social Services (RVCDSS) located on Glasco Street. I had gone to drop off paperwork for the shelter for the reimbursement of a client who had stayed one night at Angel House. Even if a woman only stays for one night, the shelter submits a reimbursement for her stay. It is not always paid, but they try.

The RVCDSS office has been fashioned out of a former YMCA and a newly constructed building adjacent to the former Y houses administrative staff. Once you have entered the building, there are two sets of double glass doors. One set of doors is not for public use; only social service staff can enter using a card swipe. The other set of doors leads to the waiting area, which is outfitted with floor-to-ceiling windows looking out onto Glasco Street, making need perceptible to passersby. From the sidewalk, row after row of people in need can be seen, sitting on plastic chairs—just waiting.

Behind a long Plexiglas window, on the left side of the room, sit frontline workers who manage client flow. The spatial design reinforces social dichotomies, rendering those at the lower end of the class system (the poor) as objects to be viewed. Those in the middle (the frontline workers) are the buffers between the poor and almost everyone else. Clients are unable to see the frontline workers because they sit in rows of chairs that do not face them. However, the frontline workers can witness all client activity. The only visual experience clients and frontline workers share is that both can see the county sheriff's office. Situating the sheriff at the RVCDSS is a design of discipline. It is not unusual to employ spatial arrangements of this sort, when the prevailing logic of power is to control people. Client oversight occurs in a range of places, including mental institutions, homeless shelters, and prisons, and constitutes a process of disciplining the "other." Components of this discipline include confinement, surveillance, and detailed organization of human action (Desjarlais 1997).

Above each Plexiglas window is a number, which designates where people are to stand based on the reason why they are there. Reading from left to right, the first is Window #4, which has a sign that reads, "Administration and Conferences." Generally the public does not go to that window, as it is reserved for people on official business with administrative staff. It is in front of Window #1 through Window #3 that most people stand. Window #3 is for Medicaid, Special Investigation, and Children's Services. Window #2 is for Food Stamps, HEAP, Lost Food Stamps, and Adult and Family Services, and Window #1 is for Public Assistance and New Photo IDs.

On the floor, approximately two feet from the window, running its length, is a strip of worn red tape. The instructions read, "DO NOT CROSS THE LINE UNTIL YOU ARE CALLED." One is notified to approach the window only after a worker has nodded his or her head. You state your name and the purpose of your visit. The prescreeners fill out an orange card, stamp it using a punch-in clock, and instruct individuals to, "sit down and we'll announce your name." When a name is called over the intercom, instructions are given to pick up one of three phones mounted on the walls. Each phone is a different color, which helps clients distinguish which one they are to pick up, so they can speak directly to a caseworker after being told to do so. As a result, conversations between recipients and caseworkers are easily overheard, and recipients, or potential recipients, often plead their cases to ensure receipt of assistance.

Because the window counters are so low, about crotch-level for someone 5'3", prescreeners rarely look at anyone standing in front of them. In fact, most of the time, frontline staff only talk to each other. It is quite humiliating to have a human being make little or no contact when you are need. It is what many of us do when we pass homeless people on the street. We look past them, hoping they will go away. This is the same experience women seeking aid were subject to.

Waiting in the Waiting Room

When I first volunteered at the shelter, Maria, the shelter director, suggested that when I was going to go to RVCDSS with women, I should always arrive before 9:00 a.m. Anybody who wants to be seen should really be there by 8:45 in the morning to wait for the doors to open. This is necessary because after 9:30 a.m., clients run the risk of not being seen at all, as the entire RVCDSS staff goes to lunch between 12:00 p.m. and 1:00 p.m., and there are no appointments taken during that hour. So, if one gets there after 9:30 a.m. with the hope of being seen before noon, that will probably not happen. But once you've entered social services, you are now on institutional time, with little or no ability to negotiate personal time constraints.

Waiting rooms, as one can imagine, are buzzing with activity. Children run around, babies cry, laugh, and are fed; adults bring breakfast, lunch, and/or snacks, because they never know how long they will have to wait. Talk and gossip abound, as people greet each other and catch up with those whom they have not seen in a while. All the talking helps to pass the time. The transparent nature of social services goes beyond the windows facing Glasco Street and the Plexiglas windows on the counter and is carried over into human interactions. Relationships are established while waiting and, on one occasion, I witnessed a relationship ending. People publicly share their hopes and dreams for jobs and housing as well as reveal aspects of their private lives. This is the backdrop to ringing phones, names being announced over the intercom system, and people pleading their cases to workers to have their benefits reinstated.

RVCDSS is primarily a woman's space, although some men do come, often just to accompany their girlfriends/wives/

sisters/cousins/nieces/friends. Frequently they come in and make sure the woman they are with is situated; they then go outside to smoke a cigarette or conduct "some business" on the pay phone. Most of the men seem to live in another world, and RVCDSS does not seem to be a part of it.

For most, there is anxiety in waiting to be seen, and people respond in different ways. Some talk to strangers, and some talk to themselves to pass the time, as they watch the clock to calculate how many minutes they have been sitting. Gloria did this while she, a shelter advocate named Jean, and I waited to see the Front End Detection System worker one Thursday morning in March 1998.

Gloria, a short, heavy-set, African-American woman with one daughter in her 20s from whom she is estranged, and one son in foster care, had come to the shelter on a Wednesday in March of 1998.[1] Gloria has a drinking problem, which is one of the reasons that her son is in foster care. The man Gloria has been living with beat her and then kicked her out of his house. Given that Gloria was now homeless the goal was to get her housed. On the day she arrived at the shelter her application had been dropped off at the River Valley County Department of Social Services to reimburse the shelter for her stay, to secure housing, and continue her food assistance. She had seen a worker the same day, Wednesday, who updated her case and informed her that she had to come back the next day, which was Thursday. She was told she would have to meet with an investigator to determine if she was eligible for housing recertification.

Gloria was petrified about being late for her appointment because the shelter volunteer who was supposed to drive us did not show up on time and Gloria really wanted to get going, and I wanted to observe my first social service interaction with a client. One of the shelter staff offered to take Gloria and asked if I wanted to go along. The drive to RVCDSS was about 5 minutes from the shelter and Gloria talked incessantly the whole time. Her conversation was full of intimate details about her life, interspersed with her fears about going to RVCDSS. She stopped talking after we parked the car and began walking toward the building. Looking scared, Gloria kept about 10 paces behind us, practically hugging the buildings as she walked.

After reaching the entrance to RVCDSS, we went directly to Window #3—Special Investigation. Gloria held on to my arm and said, "I feel faint." She registered with the prescreener and was told to wait. Since Gloria had received assistance in the past, she had to go through the Front End Detection System—FEDS. FEDS is the unit of the River Valley County Department of Social Services that investigates client fraud. I later inquired about the name FEDS, and the Codirector of Public Assistance told me, "I don't know why we call it that. I know it freaks people out, but we have to check for misuse of the system. It's a necessity."

⟶

Three circumstances flag a person going to FEDS—being single, being an immigrant, or applying for benefits if you are from outside of New York State. As a single adult, Gloria met one of the conditions that warranted investigation.

The presumption that clients are abusing social services permeates ideas about the welfare system, and Black women, in particular, have been associated with that misuse. Welfare reform underscores the belief that people abuse public benefits by implementing stringent rules, which, if not followed, results in client being sanctioned. But there is a contradictory perspective about misuse of the welfare system. One official at RVCDSS indicated that welfare reform has ushered in a new way of doing business, at least in River Valley County. The official claimed that the intense screening offers recipients faster resolution to the barriers that prevent them from working. This is accomplished by focusing on immediate needs, and quickly and efficiently directing people to the appropriate service. Supposedly, this quick response reduces the length of time a person will be on assistance. But he also indicated that welfare reform has changed the culture of administering benefits,

and the screening process sorts out those individuals who may
be trying to beat the system, making it tougher for them to do
so. He expressed the thought that with individuals being
watched more closely, a built-in intervention interrupts the tendency to abuse the system. Because of intense detection systems and close screening, people will not come to get
assistance with the idea that they're "goin' to Disney World"
with this money, he said, in a voice that mocked Black vernac-
ular. When asked if people were, in fact, fraudulent, he said
that most clients were not, noting that, "they come here with
problems and are in stressful situations." His comments were
contradictory in that the real incidence of fraud is not nearly
equal to the anxiety expressed about fraud. But directors and
employees of this bureaucratic institution seem caught up in an
ideological trap of what they know to be true and what they
think to be true. They walk a fine line because they are mandated to help people, while simultaneously debating recipients'
worthiness to receive help. This schizophrenia with regard to
welfare is weighted down by the perception that recipients
draw a "double income." Of course, concern about misuse of
funds has haunted legislators and policymakers for years.
However, as Edin and Lein (1997) point out, "getting over"
really translates into people making ends meet, because they
do not receive enough from public assistance to survive in the
first place. Historically the procedures that many women, especially Black women and women of color, went through
included investigations and interrogations used to "catch"
those engaged in fraudulent activities. Now with welfare
reform's goal of reducing the number of people on the rolls,
the ploys previously used to reduce fraudulence have been
translated into tactics of deterrence, to discourage women
from completing the application process or from trying to
maintain benefits already approved.

Gloria was distressed and even confused about having to see
the FEDS investigator. "I wonder what they're going to ask
me? I haven't done nothing wrong. I'm so nervous." From

9:15 to 10:15, while we waited, she repeated those comments again and again. I also noticed that she went to the bathroom six times.

At 10:15 a.m. a voice came over the intercom system. "Gloria Mason, please pick up the brown phone." Gloria looked at Jean and me with wide eyes and dread. She went to the phone, was instructed by the FEDS investigator to go through the doors to the left of the windows, and take the elevator to the third floor. As we walked through the doors and entered the elevator, Gloria turned to Jean and said, "Can you answer for me? I get so nervous." Jean told her that she would support her if it was necessary, but to try not to worry. We exited the elevator and walked down the corridor. When we got to the door that said Front End Detection System Office, we attempted to open the door, but could not. There are only two ways to enter any office in RVCDSS; one is to use the swipe card, and the other is to get buzzed in. We waited about 15 minutes for the investigator to buzz us in. Gloria wondered aloud what was taking so long. "I don't know why they made me come back. I ain't got nothing to hide. I ain't did nothing wrong. What do they want me for? I hope I don't get in trouble with the FEDS."

Mr. Hanson opened the door and escorted us to his office. Gloria had a panic attack. She moved so slowly that it took her about two minutes to walk 12 paces. Finally, we all entered his office and sat down. Mr. Hanson reviewed Gloria's file and then asked her address.

Mr. Hanson: What was your last place of residence?
Gloria: It was . . . I can't quite remember the numbers. Just the street.
Mr. Hanson: Do you remember where you lived before your last place of residence and who lived there with you?
Gloria: "I lived with my cousin. We had an arrangement, she and me.

Gloria had difficulty answering the questions and began fidgeting and tapping her fingers on Mr. Hanson's desk. Then she started telling him whatever came to her mind. She talked about her need for food stamps, how long she had lived with her batterer, and how he treated her. Mr. Hanson listened for a few minutes and then said he was only interested in her housing situation. Gloria continued to share random details of her life in which he had no apparent interest.

There were two recurring communication styles used by the women I accompanied to social services. The first was to tell workers almost every aspect of their lives, before they asked. In some cases, it was due to anxiety as illustrated by Gloria's experience. For other women, talking was a defense mechanism; tell everybody everything first, so they will ask you fewer questions. Just talk. If you tell them your life story, your situation, they will believe that you are not one of the people trying to "get over" on the system. In some ways, it was an attempt to exert control in a situation where there really was none. This is an issue discussed in greater detail in chapter 8.

The second communication style involved women not speaking at all or very little because it is demeaning and painful to have to justify yourself over and over again to a person with power over your life.

Upon concluding the interrogation, Mr. Hanson ended the investigation and told us we could leave. Social service time has two qualities; first, time feels like it slowed down, and second, you must live by the pace of those who work there. Simultaneously institutional time is also exaggerated, and what seems like hours with a caseworker in fact may just be minutes. Gloria experienced both, as she waited the painful hour for an investigation that lasted 8 minutes . . . all that waiting for 8 minutes.

Leaving the Building

"How long we gotta be here?" Leslie asked Paula, an advocate, one June morning. Leslie is 18 years old and pregnant. She had recently come to the shelter because her boyfriend, Dre, pushed her during an argument in the park. Leslie's head hit the jungle gym, and she made the decision that she did not want to continue living with Dre. A month before coming to the shelter, Leslie had applied for social services on her own, but had not heard back from them and desperately needed to secure Medicaid for her prenatal care. Since she had not heard from social services, she took it upon herself to go to the clinic at Smith Hospital, where she was told that she had a high-risk pregnancy and had to be careful about lifting, bending, or standing for extended periods of time. By the time Leslie arrived at the shelter, she was 6 months pregnant.

Leslie, Paula, and I arrived at RVCDSS "late"; it was 9:45 a.m. By 12:00 p.m., Leslie's name had not been announced over the loudspeaker, which meant she would have to come back after 1:00 p.m. Paula would not be able to return with us, so she asked if I would accompany Leslie. I agreed, and during the hour Leslie and I waited, she shared some things about her life, careful not to tell too much.[2] Over time Leslie confided in me even more, I suspect because she wanted an adult to look up to and has a very tense relationship with her own mother, and she knew I had a daughter her exact age. I did not take on the role of parenting her, but instead tried to act as a mentor. Leslie asked a lot of "what if questions," in an effort to get some validation for the decisions she had to make. She asked: "What if your daughter got pregnant, do you think she should still go to college?" "What if she wanted to live at home with you, would you let her?" "What if I go back to Dre?" My opinions seemed to be important to Leslie, and we began to spend more and more time together.

Part of our bond came from both of us being angry with the RVCDSS worker who was really very disrespectful to Leslie. In order to fully appreciate what happened with Ms.

Haliburton, Leslie's RVCDSS caseworker, Leslie's life story must be told. Her story also illustrates some of the problems that pregnant teenagers have as a result of welfare policy that no longer provides assistance to women 18 and under. Leslie's situation is one that expresses precisely why young women should be able to access services.

Leslie's mother Shana was 18 years old when she had Leslie. When the man who got Shana pregnant found out, he broke up with her. After Shana asked him for child support, he checked himself into a mental institution. After that, Leslie's mother formed a household with another man, whom she later married. Within 2 years, that relationship dissolved due to abuse. Shana then met another man, Paul, with whom she had the second of her three children—a girl named JoJo. For a while they lived in Laneville and then moved to Ohio to be near Paul's family. Shana did not get along with Paul's family and left while still pregnant, and returned to Laneville, leaving Leslie with Paul and his family. Leslie missed her mother terribly and recalls being badly treated by Paul's family. They never gave her gifts at holidays and pinched her to wake her in the morning. When speaking with her mother on the phone, family members snatched the phone from Leslie as soon as she inquired when Shana was going to come back.

After JoJo's birth Leslie and Paul moved back to Laneville, but the family unit disintegrated when Shana discovered Paul had been with another woman. She took the children and moved to a homeless shelter.

Several years later, Leslie, her mother, and JoJo moved in with another man, who fathered Shana's third child, Michael. They did not live with Michael's father for the duration of the pregnancy because Shana then met James. James moved in with Shana and her children after being released from jail. On his first night he locked Leslie and her sister JoJo in the bedroom and beat Shana. Shortly after Michael was born, Shana gave her two youngest children to their respective fathers, while she and Leslie continued to live with James, who was abusive to both of them.

Throughout her young life, Leslie has experienced abandonment, psychological, sexual, and physical abuse. Then just before completing high school, Shana told Leslie that she did not want her to live with her anymore. Leslie joined a Job Corps Program in Upstate New York where she obtained her GED and completed vocational training. After completing the program, she moved back in with her mother. Her return was met with hostility and more physical violence:

> One day I left a spoon in the sink and me and my mother started arguing and fighting and she tried to throw me out with no clothes on. My uncle took me to live with him. But I went back to my mother's after a week and then she took me to Brooklyn to live with my father, who was staying with his sister. When we got there, he wasn't around and his sister said she didn't know anything about me living with them. I went back to my mom's house and we got into more fights. I packed my things and told her I was moving to The Haven [a shelter for homeless youth.] When the staff asked her if she wanted me back, she said no.
>
> I was in the independent living program, working and sharing an apartment with a roommate. But after awhile, I didn't like the rules anymore. So I left and moved in with a friend. Me and my friend stopped going to work and started doing illegal activities like selling drugs. I did it for a couple of months, but I finally realized that wasn't the life for me. I moved back into my uncle's house, where I was like the nanny to his kids. I got tired of raising his children and moved to my aunt's house. I stayed with her until I was accepted into the army.

Shortly before Leslie joined the army, she met Dre, who visited her frequently at the base, and after 8 months Leslie became pregnant:

I was sent home from the army (because of my pregnancy) and I went to live with Dre. We used to fight a
lot but it wasn't physical except that time in the park.
So, I moved into the shelter. Me and Dre are in counseling working on our relationship but I still live at
the shelter. I am now six months pregnant. I don't
really know where my life is headed next, but I hope
it takes a turn for the better.

Leslie's story is an extreme example of a life riddled with
events over which she had no control. She has no money, no
health care, and one of the thinnest social support networks of
all of the women I met and, to make matters worse, as a
teenager she had little entitlement to public assistance.

The 1996 Welfare Reform Law contains provisions affect-
ing teenage mothers.[3] The new legislation requires that minor
mothers live with a parent or legal guardian in order to receive
benefits, a policy shift that emerged in response to public fears
about teenage mothers "draining" society.[4] In reality, the
actual numbers of teenage pregnancies, according to the Alan
Guttmacher Institute (1999), have decreased in the two
decades from 1970 to 1990. But the issue of teenage pregnancy is often conflated with concern about out-of-wedlock
births. In spite of the distinctions between the two (teen pregnancy does not necessarily mean out-of-wedlock and out-of-
wedlock does not predominantly occur among teens, but
rather, among adult women), it is teenage pregnancy that has
been depicted as the major problem. It is really public anxiety
about the supposed "immorality" of young women's sexual
behavior that has led to the denigration of teen mothers and
has served as the driving force behind the adoption of more
punitive measures for those who need public assistance
(Polakow 1999b). Conservatives take the position that teenage
pregnancy violates family norms; welfare reform policies therefore reflect that position. Thus, virtually all government assistance to pregnant teenagers has now been eliminated.

The public picture of teenage pregnancy has been highly distorted. Teen mothers are depicted as milking the welfare system, as if they alone are to blame for "out of control" public spending. The assumption is that to be a pregnant teen means that one is inherently loose and hypersexual. Politicians' and the media's constructions of teenage pregnancy as an epidemic rarely mention that fewer pregnancies occur among young women (age 15 to 17) than among those who are 18 to 19, who are theoretically adults (Luker 1991). The birthrate among teenagers from 15 to 17 in New York State is 26 per 1,000 but among those 18 to 19 the rate is 66 per 1,000 (Alan Guttmacher Institute 1999). More importantly, studies have shown that the younger the girl is when she has sex, the more likely it is that her first sexual experience was not voluntary (Child Trends 1997).

Young women face a number of difficulties similar to Leslie's, and teenage pregnancy cannot be simply reduced to a matter of young girls' sexual amorality (Polakow 1993; Seccombe 1999). Rather, teenage pregnancy is a complicated issue that cannot be resolved by demonizing young women.

Leslie and I returned to RVCDSS at 1:00 p.m. Shortly after our arrival, Leslie was summoned to pick up one of the phones and was told to wait by the door to be buzzed into the caseworkers' office area. Ms. Haliburton came out to escort us to her office. She was very pleasant while examining Leslie's case file. "Let's see now, Leslie," she said quickly looking at the personal information portion of the application, "You are how old?" "I'm 18," replied Leslie. "I see you're staying at the Angel House." Leslie did not answer. "Oh, I see, you are pregnant and you were in the army. What are your plans for the future? Maybe after you've had the baby you can pick up where you left off." She reviewed the case file quietly and in short order said, "I'm sorry but I can't open a case for you. You're underage. You're not eligible for any services. Do you have any family?" Leslie replied in a soft voice, "Yes, my mother lives in Ohio, but we fight all the time." "Well, dear, children fight with their parents all the time. My son and I fought when he was your age. It's all a part of growing up," said Ms. Haliburton. Just then the phone rang, and she reached to pick it up. Leslie used this break in Ms. Haliburton's incorrect assessment of her life to roll her eyes and whispered, "What am I gonna do?" I said, "I think you might explain to her what fighting means."

Ms. Haliburton ended her phone conversation and launched right into a discussion about what Leslie's options were. She made it clear that the only assistance Leslie could receive was a one-way ticket to her mother's house in Ohio and $5 to buy food along the way. "Is that what you want to do?" I asked. Leslie looked petrified and responded that she didn't know. "Can I have a few days to think it over? When would I have to leave?" Ms. Haliburton informed Leslie that she could not think about it for a day or two; she would have to leave immediately, meaning within 24 hours. Ms. Haliburton told us that she would be right back; she was going to get the $5 for Leslie's trip. I had wanted to interject, but she moved too quickly. When she returned, she gave Leslie the $5 and asked her to sign a receipt acknowledging receipt of the money and that she would use it for the stated purpose of buying food on her trip to Ohio. Ms. Haliburton then picked up the phone and called a bus company to find out the cost of the ticket. She asked what town her mother lived in while waiting to be connected to a service representative. I urged Leslie to tell Ms. Haliburton about her relationship with her mother. "I just want to leave," Leslie said. "She's telling me I have no choice, so I guess it's better than nothing." Then I suggested to Leslie that she ask to see the domestic violence liaison. After having found out the bus schedule, Ms. Haliburton got off the phone and Leslie said, "I want to see the violence lady."

🕭

Yvonne Genesee is River Valley County's Domestic Violence Liaison who implements the Family Violence Option (FVO) which ensures that battered recipients receive some exemptions from the punitive aspects of the law. Yvonne assesses the credibility of an applicants' claim to determine the need for waivers from employment or from seeking child support; to provide emergency safety planning; and then, to reassess a case after the waiver period has been reached. Yvonne can recommend that a victim be granted a waiver from some or all of the requirements and still receive aid. In Leslie's case, she could have determined whether or not Leslie had to go live with her mother.

Yvonne is a warm, friendly woman who takes her job very seriously. When we met in February of 1999, she expressed satisfaction that the program was successful. Her major trepidation was that some caseworkers had not been appropriately trained to screen applicants for domestic violence.[5] This was a national concern that was not unwarranted, evidenced by an analysis of Wisconsin's welfare program (known as W–2), which found that domestic violence victims were overlooked, and W–2 caseworkers frequently failed to advise women of available support services, program options, or exemptions from certain regulations (Center for Law and Social Policy 2000). According to Yvonne 400 women in River Valley County had indicated on their applications that they were victims of domestic violence, and she granted just about 200 waivers, mostly for child support, relieving women of having to force the fathers of their children to pay. Other waivers exempted women from having to work for an average of 4 months.[6]

Early assessments of the FVO suggested that the option has not proved effective in helping current victims obtain enough time off from the requirements, nor have enough women been able to obtain the support services they need (Raphael 1999). My critique of the Family Violence Option is that race is not viewed as a variable in assessing how well it does or does not work. For example, a collaborative study by the NOW Legal Defense and Education Fund, The Legal Aid Society, Civil Division, the Urban Justice Center, and the Women, Welfare and Abuse Task Force (Hearn 2000) sought to determine whether welfare applicants in New York City were being screened for domestic violence. The research found that clients and potential clients were not informed about services available for domestic violence victims. The report also showed that of those who took the survey, most welfare applicants and recipients had not received the domestic violence screening form. Fifty-eight percent of the participants reported that they were not referred to a liaison, and 88% were not informed about the Family Violence Option waivers when they first applied for assistance. While the report provides an important critique of the FVO, it fails to offer an analysis of the findings based on race and ethnicity to determine whether there are any differences in women's ability to use the Option. When I raised this issue, I was told that most of the welfare recipients in New York City are Black and Latina, anyway. Repudiating the importance of analyzing data by race may be viewed as a dismissal of its centrality in understanding the ways in which racism is structured. Moreover, lack of attention to race exemplifies the reification of color blindness, making it more difficult to point out the consequences of racism. We may view this as a form of racism, although it is muted because there is no direct reference made to race (Davis 2004). Yet its absence in the context of a society in which race continues to structure people's life chances is an anathema.

Leslie represents the second example of how Black women in this study were unable to access the Domestic Violence Liaison. Sherita, whose situation is described in chapter 1, was not directed to talk to Yvonne, even though she indicated she experienced violence on her assistance application. Despite universal availability, notification about the Family Violence Option was not evenly shared.

One possible explanation for this uneven access to the Family Violence Option is that Black women are rarely viewed as victims of violence because historically they have been viewed as virtueless. James (1996) contends that this is one reason that various types of violence against Black women are not addressed by the state; Black women are seen as having little value. A similar argument is made by Ammons (1995), who notes how ineffective the battered women's syndrome is as a defense in court for Black women charged with murdering their abusers because those in judgment do not believe Black women can be victimized. Their analyses shore up the real life situation described by Barbee (n.d.). Barbee claims that violence in the Black community is viewed as normative and offers a personal account to make her point. She describes being attacked by a Black man in a public venue and having passersby ignore her calls for help. She had the opportunity to ask one woman why she ignored her plea, and the woman replied that she thought they were together. Barbee's interpretation of this response is that people believe that violence within Black relationships is normal and acceptable.

Black women who experience violence are bound by constraints of unworthiness in relation to victim services. The issue of battered women's ability to secure resources if they are on welfare becomes more complex because their status as victims of violence is reined in by race. Little sympathy is summoned up to ensure Black women's protection. Seemingly the negativity that shrouds poor Black women, evidenced by their persistent ineligibility for aid from the 1900s to the 1960s, is similar to that which reduces their credibility as victims of violence.

After my prompt, Leslie asked again to see the domestic violence liaison. Her request was denied. "The Violence Lady?" Ms. Haliburton said, with a frown on her face. At this point, Leslie was exasperated and quite angry. Ms. Haliburton then accused Leslie of wanting to get out of moving to Ohio. It sounded "suspicious," she said. After all, Ms. Haliburton argued, Leslie had not mentioned parental abuse during the earlier part of the conversation. The discussion only "came up" after arrangements were being made for Leslie to get on the bus. Now she was bringing up domestic violence as an issue. I whispered to Leslie to tell Ms. Haliburton about her mother's abuse but Leslie said to me, "You tell her, I'm too mad."

Turning to Ms. Haliburton I said, "She tried to tell you earlier that she and her mother fought. She did not mean they had arguments, they fought. She doesn't want to live with her father because he has mental health issues. She wants to see the domestic violence liaison because she is not sure Ohio is where she should be." Ms. Haliburton was visibly annoyed and told Leslie that she'd better think about what she had said because the charge of parental abuse is very serious. Did she have any records of charges? Had she told any authority? If so, then she could see the domestic violence liaison. After what sounded like a verbal assault, Leslie turned toward me and said, "I'm leaving."

Continuing to perform her adversarial role, Ms. Haliburton said as we left, "If you don't pick up your bus ticket, you have to return the $5." We left RVCDSS, and Leslie cursed Ms. Haliburton the whole walk back to the shelter. When we arrived at the shelter, I told Maria, the shelter director, what had happened. She was just as appalled as I was and asked me to fill out a human rights monitoring report, to document Leslie's mistreatment.[7] I asked Leslie if she felt her rights to information about and access to services had been violated, and she responded, "Yes, it seemed like the lady wasn't hearing anything I said, she was rushing me. I might be eligible for Medicaid or food stamps, but I won't know from her." I filled out the form and gave Leslie a copy. Meanwhile, Maria called Ms. Haliburton's supervisor making the point that it would be dangerous for Leslie to be forced to live with her mother. Subsequently, the initial denial for assistance was reversed, and Leslie was given a budget for a rental, food stamp allotment, and Medicaid. Because she was getting her needs met through the state, Leslie was also subjected to the work requirements and was told she had to see an employment counselor. This interaction will be discussed in the next chapter.

The diversionary approaches of welfare reform have contributed to the national decrease in welfare caseloads. Prying into women's lives is an old tactic to keep women from receiving aid, but it takes on an ironic twist when one considers that the goal of welfare reform policy is to move recipients toward "self-sufficiency." How is it possible to achieve this when the economic support that is so often necessary is denied? And, although the Family Violence Option is an effort intended to accommodate the needs of domestic violence victims, the pressure to decrease caseloads overshadows the purpose of the option.

Gloria and Leslie were assessed during the application process against a logic that really sought to reduce the welfare rolls, not a logic that sought to provide them with resources. They were viewed in the waiting rooms, interrogated in inner offices, and dismissed as fraudulent subjects because they needed assistance. Leslie felt betrayed by these presumptions and could not quite reconcile why Ms. Haliburton would sabotage her effort to live without violence. Gloria and Leslie's interactions with investigators and caseworkers at RVCDSS mirror the experiences other women had when they applied or reapplied for social services, particularly women of color. It is clear that women experience roadblocks in their quest for Safety Net and TANF funding, even when the grievous circumstance of violence is taken into account. Battered women have the history of a movement that has sensitized the public about violence. Against this backdrop, along with the Family Violence Option, we might expect them to have a somewhat easier time securing welfare. But this is not the case. It makes one wonder, what women, who do not reveal their abuse or those who are not battered, are up against.

Parallels may be made between being engaged with social services and being victimized by violence. Neil Websdale, in his book, *Policing the Poor*, (2001) explains the techniques batterers use to control women. He notes that "domestic violence is a means for men to control women and to exercise their power over them. It involves coercion and threats; intimidation through looks, gestures, actions; isolation including stringent surveillance and regulation of what a woman does . . ." (132). Gloria, Leslie, and other women experienced ceremonies of degradation when they went to the social services office. For they too were investigated, deterred, intimidated, and denied access to services, among other things. Some of the women were revictimized by the social services institution.

Their revictimization was inflected with race. Some caseworker interactions and practices are choreographed around broader tensions about Black women on welfare, regardless of their status as victims of violence. Interestingly, welfare reform policy almost perfectly interprets societal angst about Black women: they can justifiably be treated with disrespect and caution based on the imagined societal destruction they cause or the fraud they might commit. The very "possibility" that these transgressions might occur authorizes increased surveillance and deterrence, which may be seen as blurring the line between poverty and criminality.

No Magic in the Market

Mandatory Work and Training Programs

The cornerstones of the Personal Responsibility and Work Reconciliation Act of 1996 (PRWORA) are by now well-known. Its most stringent directive is the requirement that people on welfare work or be engaged in work-related activities, a mandate that was proposed as a panacea to force the poor into the nation's economic mainstream. In New York State the PRWORA was articulated in terms of three goals, which were: 1) to increase employment among the state's most economically needy families, including welfare recipients and former recipients; 2) to reduce teen-age pregnancy, out of wedlock births, and the rising numbers of children living in single-parent families; and 3) to reduce dependency on government assistance for economic support (New York State Office of Temporary Disability Assistance, 1999). The New York State Welfare Reform Act of 1997 packaged these goals as a twofold message: to recipients of public assistance the message was that one should work, not rely on welfare. To bureaucrats the message was to emphasize workforce participation rather than welfare eligibility. Thus TANF, the program for women with children, and Safety Net, the program for single adults, both require that recipients of benefits must work under specific terms (Leibschutz 2000).

Broadly speaking, the idea is that with employment, people would no longer need welfare. At the very least, it was believed the need for public assistance would decrease, as wages were garnered in the formal wage-labor market. If recipients cannot immediately become attached to work, which may be either subsidized or unsubsidized through so-called workfare programs, then they must participate in work-related activities, including community service, educational or vocational training, and other job readiness activities. Noncompliance results in sanctioning; that is, the denial of benefits for a certain time period or case closure. In chapter 2, the point was made that battered women's advocates challenged the work mandate on the grounds that patterns of violence would interfere with women's employment. Elaborating on that point, other research suggests that women's partners sometimes sabotage their efforts toward economic independence by injuring them and/or preventing them from successfully meeting work or work-related activity requirements (Raphael and Tolman 1997; Brandwein 1999). One example comes from Passaic County, New Jersey. In a study showing that 39.7% of women in a welfare-to-work training program were abused, women explicitly stated that their partners tried to prevent them from obtaining training, threatened by their possible autonomy (Curcio 1997). Also, the health problems associated with violence, such as visible bruises and Post Traumatic Stress Disorder, compromise battered women's ability to work and suggests the possible ongoing need for public assistance. Ultimately, these obstacles must be acknowledged as factors that may force women to stay with or return to their batterers. In the former situation, women may give up and resign themselves to their partners' sabotage. In the latter circumstance, women may return to their batterers, unable to meet the work obligations for health reasons, thereby precipitating case closure and pushing them deeper into poverty. Once women leave the rolls, they are evidence of the "success" of welfare policy, regardless of the actual reasons why women left welfare. No doubt, these concerns about welfare reform as they relate to physical violence are certainly well substantiated and cause for alarm. As harmful and horrific as direct physical violence is, few critiques of welfare reform policy examine how components of the policy are also forms of violence. Specifically forcing people to work or enter training programs, knowing that the work is low-wage, and limiting assistance, should in fact, be interpreted as a revictimization of vulnerable women in the public sphere.

The imperative to examine welfare reform policy in relation to marketplace mania is important because of River Valley County's economic circumstance, which mimicked that of many other communities across the United States. There were precipitous decreases in major manufacturing industries, and rises in technology and the service sectors have had a push-pull effect, where local governments must both contain economic erosion and simultaneously devise revitalization schemes. At the intersection of these phenomena are poor and working-class people receiving public assistance, for whom economic security is uncertain and often unattainable. Through the experience of Black women who are battered, who are on welfare, and who now must participate in work programs, we see how impoverishment is related to labor regimes imposed as part of the new global economy that depends on low-wage workers (Morgen and Maskovsky 2003: 318). Policies that require those in need of social welfare to work or receive training in low-level employment reproduce the existing division of labor, which is a hierarchy of inequality organized along the axis of gender and race.

This chapter considers three aspects of welfare reform's work mandate in relation to battered Black women living in the city of Laneville. It begins by exploring changes in the area's economy during the early 1990s, paying particular attention to the county's manufacturing sector and the effects of corporate downsizing in this community. Following this is one case study that exemplifies the relationship between the county's economic interests and the work mandate of welfare policy. In this situation the microtactics of control that directed one woman toward low-wage work, are documented. Lastly, I provide a second case study to illustrate how women are guided toward training (a form of work-related activity) that leads only to low-wage work. The latter two reflect the not-so-invisible mechanisms through which race and gender are ordered in relation to policy and constitute both regulation and structural violence.

Deindustrialization in River Valley County

River Valley County underwent many changes in the 1980s to 1990s just before welfare reform legislation was passed and has performed the balancing act of revitalizing its local economy, responding to devolution (the process of shifting federal responsibility of social programs to individual states), and meeting the federal government's requirement that TANF and Safety Net populations receive benefits in exchange for working. As expected, these factors influenced the workforce development activities of River Valley County, with implications for poor people on welfare who, as a vulnerable group, may be viewed as a source of labor to meet local business needs. In other words, local governments can use their welfare population to meet promises made to various business sectors.

In the 1940s the Zytron Corporation opened a manufacturing plant in the Town of Laneville. Over the next 50 years, the corporation grew both fiscally and physically, garnering revenues of $69 billion and expanding not only to other municipalities in River Valley but also to nearby counties in the upstate region. Employee growth increased from 350 in the 1940s to approximately 30,000 people by the late 1980s, representing a little less than 20 percent of Zytron's worldwide employees. Big "Z", as it is known, was the largest private employer in the county followed by the River Valley County Government. As a major manufacturer that matured and incorporated technology, Zytron faced little competition and perpetuated "a job for life" image.

The company was the preferred place of employment for several women in this study, although only one, Sherita, had actually worked there. If you will recall, she relocated to Laneville and worked for Zytron as an administrative assistant before getting laid off, which is what happened to thousands of others when the company downsized.

Despite stellar growth, in 1991 Zytron posted its first ever loss of $1.4 million and responded by reducing its regional workforce in River Valley and other neighboring counties, by 2,000 people. However, this plan to decrease the workforce was not viewed with great alarm to people living in the upstate region because Zytron had a policy of job security and full employment. Reductions came mostly in the form of voluntary departures, and although 20% of the company's worldwide workforce was located in the upstate region, only 7% of Zytron Corp's worldwide workforce was located in River Valley County. Some argued that the county could handle the job loss, assuming that former "Z" workers would be absorbed into smaller manufacturing firms. The problem was that manufacturing was no longer the region's economic draw; technology was. Additionally, other major local employers, such as the River Valley County government, psychiatric centers, hospitals, the Postal Service, and a nearby correctional facility, which cumulatively employed over 9,000 people, were pressured to trim their staffs. By 1992 the impact of the combined layoffs from Zytron and other major employers contributed to a county unemployment rate of 7.1%.

Early in 1992 Zytron restructured, which included the elimination of 25,000 jobs worldwide. In late 1992 Zytron stated that it intended to eliminate an additional 3,500 jobs, for a total of 5,500. The announcement was so alarming that the *Laneville Journal* set up a telephone hotline to keep residents appraised of Zytron news. The *Journal* even altered its layout format to accommodate analyses of Zytron Corp's pending cuts. One Wednesday in the winter of 1993, Big "Z" officials announced its expected layoffs, and 6,000 jobs were eliminated at three plants in the upstate region. By June 1993 the county's unemployment rate rose to 11.2%, the worst in New York State. In fact, this was the worst unemployment rate in the 24 years that such statistics had been kept. In addition to driving up unemployment, Zytron's downsizing shrank the upstate region's tax base and consequently reduced spending. Low reemployment rates in the county prevailed, due to the inability to absorb former Zytron employees. By December of 1994 there was a cumulative loss of 11,500 jobs in River

Valley County. While things improved somewhat by 1999, when overall county unemployment was 3.9%, Black unemployment was more than double that at 8.9%, the highest rate of any minority group, suggesting that it was this group that was facing the most barriers to reemployment.

Clearly the county had overrelied on one corporation, and the corrective was to diversify the economic base. The strategy adopted involved marketing former Zytron properties to companies in similar industries. The River Valley County Economic Development Corporation (RVCEDC) went into high gear to transform its previously dependent relationship with Big "Z" and its image (River Valley County Economic Development Corporation 1999). Using economic forecasts to identify future labor needs, local economists recommended that the county focus on five areas of business development. The first four were high-tech manufacturing, information systems, agriculture, and tourism. Of course high-tech manufacturing and information systems development made a lot of sense because those who had been laid off from Zytron could be reskilled to work in these industries. Enough mid- and upper-level professionals were out of work to fill positions in small companies, and the idea was that several small companies, with 50 employees or less, were better for the economy than one company monopolizing all the human capital in a given area. If one or two companies closed down, the impact of unemployment would be less severe. Despite losses in its industrial base, River Valley sold itself. The marketing plan was so well executed that the RVCEDC won an award for its creativity in attracting, retaining and expanding business, developing the workforce, and promoting tourism.

It was however, the fifth sector that was forecasted to outpace all of those mentioned above, and that was the service sector, jobs requiring only on-the-job, informal, or vocational training. Sassen-Koob (1983) explains that when cities lose their industrial base, they often become producers of services rather than goods, although this process is generally applied to a few critically located cities like New York and Los Angeles. These jobs include service supervisors, private household workers, and data processing, office machine, and communications equipment operators. They also include clerical occupations, protective services, food service, health service, cleaning and building service, and personal service.[1] According to the New York State Department of Labor, total projected job growth by educational and training requirement in the upstate region would be highest for those who completed *vocational training or job-related courses that did not result in a degree* but could be combined with on-the-job training. A workforce would be needed to meet the anticipated largest occupational growth areas: retail trade, health, business, and educational services.[2] All of these jobs have high turnover rates (an indicator of low training requirements and/or low average earnings). And some members of this workforce were recruited from the population of TANF and Safety Net assistance recipients, most of whom lived in Laneville, who were bound under new rules to be employed or participating in an employment-related activity. This meant they were a particularly vulnerable group, capable of being easily exploited.

Pushed into the Service of the Service Economy

Leslie, the 18-year old pregnant African-American woman discussed in the previous chapter, had a second meeting with Ms. Haliburton, her caseworker at social services, 2 weeks after the first meeting in early June. Ms. Haliburton was cold and curt, speaking through clenched teeth, undoubtedly because her supervisor reprimanded her for not permitting Leslie to see Yvonne Genesee, the domestic violence liaison, upon request. When they met again Ms. Haliburton informed Leslie that she was eligible for Medicaid after having initially told her she was not. She also informed Leslie that she had to work if she were to receive income support, and an appointment had been made for Leslie to speak with Ms. Pauli, a River Valley County Department of Social Services employment counselor, that very day.

After finding our way to her cubicle, Ms. Pauli began laying out the rules of engagement—Leslie would have to come back to the office every other week until she found employment. She was expected to go on five job interviews per week and log the outcome of those interviews in a little booklet; if she failed to bring in the booklet, missed an appointment, or refused a position offered to her, she could lose her benefits. After finding employment, her employer would have to submit Leslie's timesheet to RVCDSS to verify her work compliance. Leslie placed her hand on her stomach and said to Ms. Pauli: "I was told by the doctors at the clinic not to lift anything heavy or do too much standing or walking. I have a high-risk pregnancy. Can I get a medical waiver?" Leslie's medical issues were of little concern to Ms. Pauli, as she quickly pulled out a copy of an employment newspaper and began reading job listings aloud. "There is a job at Home Depot. Here's another one for a cashier at one of the shops at the Mall. Can you get to the Mall?" Both of the positions Ms. Pauli recommended required travel as well as long periods of standing on one's feet—two things Leslie did not think she could physically tolerate. Furthermore, Leslie did not believe anyone would hire her, given that she was now 7 months pregnant. The job listings Ms. Pauli read off did not interest Leslie; they were low-paying and offered no opportunity for advancement. Leslie also said the physical requirements, having to stand and lift things, would be a problem.

But then, Ms. Pauli was not primarily concerned with Leslie's health. She only stressed that Leslie must regularly bring in her job search card with the required number of signatures indicating she had looked for employment. Since Leslie did not like the options presented to her, she made an appointment with a gentleman she had seen sitting at a desk in RVCDSS's waiting area. Michael Wells worked for the Private Industry Council's[3] welfare-to-work program and coordinated job searches for social service clients. Within a week, Mr. Wells had identified possible employment and set up an interview. Leslie was hired temporarily at the YWCA working 5 hours a day, 5 days a week running around after other people's children, basically providing day care. She took the job because she believed it was the only way she could qualify for benefits, and she thought it was the lesser of the evils among the other employment options Ms. Pauli told her about. At least she might be able to sit down part of the time she worked.

Two weeks after she began her job, Leslie and I met up and went for a walk. She did not bring up the job at first, instead sharing that she still had morning sickness and that it never seemed to stop, not even in her 7th month of pregnancy. Finally, I asked how the job was going, and she said it was "all right" but she wasn't making a lot of money. In fact, the amount of money she made was so embarrassing that Leslie refused to tell me how much she earned. All she said was: "I've never made so little money in my life. Please don't ask me what I bring home. I'll tell you it's not enough to get a place to live or do anything. I can't even afford to buy lunch each day. I certainly won't be able to save to get things for the baby." I pressed the issue just a little and asked if she brought home less than $200 every two weeks to which she replied, "Yes," but offered no further information. I suspect Leslie made about $5.25 per hour amounting to $262.50 every two weeks. After taxes, she probably had a take-home pay of $175. In preparation for her baby's arrival, Leslie had planned to use her money to purchase some items, but after transportation to get to and from work (she sometimes had to take a cab because her legs hurt) and the cost of buying food for lunch, very little was left to purchase anything for the baby. In fact on this day she only had $4.50. As we walked back to the shelter we stopped at a take-out restaurant. The chicken and biscuit lunch she wanted cost $5.25, but Leslie only had $4.50. Embarrassed that she did not have enough money to pay for the meal, after having ordered it, I offered to pay.

One month later, in August when she was 8 months pregnant, Leslie's job ended. By then a TANF budget had been approved; $347 for an apartment, $121.28 for food stamps, and $388 in cash. Some of the cash was withheld, for reasons which were unclear. It may have represented the calculated difference between the approved amount and her earned income from her job at the camp, which Leslie no longer received, since the summer program had ended. Instead of $388, Leslie received $125, an amount she was told had to last her until the end of September or early October, after the birth.

In addition to trying to live off of $125 after having met the work mandate, welfare reform requirements continued to haunt her. In a ceaseless effort to keep her working, social services informed Leslie that she had to find yet another job and work until she gave birth. One Friday night I visited Leslie, and she was visibly worried: "You know those people at social services want me to get another job and work until the baby is born? They've sent me lots of letters about coming in. What kinda job am I going to get for a couple of weeks being 8 months pregnant?" When I asked her what she was going to do for money she said:

> Well I am babysitting for a lady who paid me $5 yesterday and $4 today. I can't believe it, they keep sending me letters about working and telling me I am missing appointments. I'm not going to see them, I *am* working. How can I go in for an appointment when I'm making some money [doing babysitting]?

Leslie made $9 for 2 days of work watching the children of another woman who was receiving TANF funding and had to go to work and whose child care had fallen through. Of course there is no way the money Leslie made could be considered sufficient, but in the face of social services micromanaging her work life, Leslie wrested some control away from the system. She willingly accepted $9 to avoid being under the watchful eye of her caseworker and was able to live some part of her "welfared" life on her own terms.

Women took jobs reflecting Laneville's new economy. Of the 13 Black women interviewed, 11 were told they had to find employment by RVCDSS workers, or they faced losing their benefits. Eight out of the 11 found work in low-paying jobs offering no employment security. At no point did any Black woman interviewed, who was mandated to work in order to receive assistance, make enough money to survive. White women on the other hand had different experiences. Although I did not formerly interview Lorraine, a 30-something-year-old White woman with two children who left her abusive husband, I accompanied her to the Department of Social Services. She discussed with the caseworker how important it was for her to stay home with her children, and how much she was looking forward to getting their lives settled. The caseworker was so enthusiastic about helping Lorraine and supported her plans, at least while we were in the office. It was amazing that the caseworker never mentioned to Lorraine that she would have to work.

Others however, staved off being sanctioned and scrambled for jobs. When job fairs were held, women rushed off from the shelter, with their children in tow to find jobs working as flexible laborers. They vied for the same positions as fast-food workers, child-care workers, home-health aids, and in retail—all low-paying. They were excluded from jobs that could have paid higher wages because they were unable to access training or education that would have enhanced their skills. And although some educational opportunities exist, none of the Black women were aware of them. Lack of access to education and training constitutes one form of structural violence because opportunity for social and economic mobility is intentionally restricted. Indeed, the ability to survive is restricted to the degree that getting what one needs (i.e., foodstamps) is tied to compulsory activity.

Restricted occupational choice has historically circumscribed Black women, and with few other options they have worked primarily as domestics and service workers (Harley 2002). At the time of Emancipation, Black women workers were primarily situated in such service jobs as domestic workers, servants, laundresses, cooks, and nurses. In the early 1900s, having been barred from nearly all jobs other than service work, approximately 44% of African-American women were employed as domestic servants or laundresses (Amott and Matthaei, 1991). Black women's work represents the dialectic of achievement and constraint. At particular moments, such as during World Wars I and II, small numbers of Black women benefited from work in war-related industries in ship and rail yards, munitions plants, and the like. Yet they experienced occupational controls as "the most disposable segment of the American labor force" (Harley 2002: 4). They therefore experienced higher rates of job loss in occupational sectors that are segregated and are at the lowest rung of the economic ladder.

Between 1950 and 1980 Black women went from being farm workers and servants to being service and clerical workers, reflecting larger economic changes, as the United States moved from an industrial to a service economy. The service economy has proliferated with the expansion of the finance, insurance, and real estate industries with a concomitant contraction of factory work.[4] While the service sector does, in fact, include some high wage positions such as dental hygienists and nurses, these are employment categories requiring higher skill levels, and gender and race demarcate which groups are more likely to have access to those jobs. Black women's participation in service work continued through the 1970s and 1980s, with one in four Black women in the service sector compared to one out of every six White women (Harley, et al. 2002).

In 1995, 1.7 million Black women were employed in the service sector (United States Department of Labor 1997). Although employment options expanded as a consequence of increased educational attainment, Black women were still clustered into and overrepresented into three occupational groups used by the U.S. Department of Labor: managerial and professional, technical sales and administrative support, and the service sector. In the twenty-first century, according the United States Department of Labor (2001a, 2001b) 25% of Black women or 2 million, were employed in service occupations compared to 16% of White women in 2001. Although Black women have historically participated in the labor force to a greater degree than White women, the gap in labor force participation narrowed in the 1990s. Then in 1997 the gap increased, as Black women's labor force participation began to once again rise more rapidly than White women's (Cantave and Harrison 1999). One cannot help but link the widening gap to the fact that the 1996 Welfare Reform bill pushed one class of Black women—poor Black women—into the workforce through mandatory work. The question of course remains, what is the nature of that work?

Black women's continuous relegation to service sector jobs was clear among those interviewed in 1999, as they worked in or trained for positions that were really extensions of Black women's historical occupational roles. What is unique about the continuation of this employment trend in the twenty-first century is how neoliberal ideology and shifts in the economy facilitate participation in this sector by driving people to be dependent upon low-wage jobs (Davis 2004).

Some economists have argued that labor markets are sex-typed and segregated by race and ethnicity. "Thus, jobs in the labor force hierarchy tend to be simultaneously race-typed and gender-typed. Almost all jobs tend to be typed in such a way that stereotypes make it difficult for persons of the 'wrong' race and/or gender to train for or obtain the job" (Amott and Matthaei, 1991: 24).

Black women's workforce participation in River Valley County is no different than national trends and did not flow beyond the service sector into other occupational categories. The persistent patterns of occupational segmentation show up in Census reports. In 1990 African-American women in River Valley County made up 3.1% of the labor force and were overrepresented in the service sector, of which they made up 8% of the labor force. They were employed in that sector more than in any other. Ten years later, in the 2000 Census, African-American women in River Valley County made up 3.3% of the labor force and 7.5% of those were employed in the service sector, again more than in any other.

Where race intersects with gendered occupational segmentation in which loss of industry is the backdrop, we find that women who are compelled to work (due to mandatory work requirements) do not earn enough to survive. Unable to achieve economic security through low-wage employment, women are pushed to make choices that increase their vulnerability to harm in order to survive economically. Gina, a young African-American woman who was not formerly interviewed, but with whom I spent time, made nowhere near the amount of money needed to cover her expenses, commenting that: "I work at the supermarket as a cashier. Eighteen hours a week, three days from 7 a.m. to 1 p.m., and not enough money is made. $92.70. I get $45 in food stamps a month and my rent budget is for $375. I'll have to get a second job to take care of things." Unable to cobble together a cumulative living wage from a number of service jobs and the constant threat of having her Safety Net funding cut, Gina told Leslie she was considering working in a strip club in order to make more money. She would lap dance, she said, or take on "customers"; whatever it took to survive. Another young woman, Joelle, received limited assistance and worked two jobs, one at McDonald's (the job she reported to her caseworker) and the other selling drugs. Both Gina and Joelle were at risk of criminalization because they lacked adequate resources.

As poor Black women, finding permanent full-time employment paying a living wage in Laneville was a pipe dream. Leslie, Gina, and Joelle lived the reality that economic sufficiency could not be secured with low wages in an economic environment in which downsizing, outsourcing, and contingent labor were the norm. What would make a difference to almost all the women with whom I spoke was having access to a meaningful education. Women were well aware that education was a far more reasonable approach to finding good jobs and knew that a college degree would increase their income and career opportunities. And although River Valley County supports some programs at community colleges, it does not permit recipients to achieve a two-year Associates degree. Leslie for example, wanted to return to school but instead had to accept being a child-care worker. Sherita also wanted to attend college to become a social worker and

thought that obtaining her Associates Degree would put her in
a position to do so, but instead was directed to a training program to become a certified nursing assistant.

Training for Low Wages

Women's educational goals were sometimes mismatched
against what RVCDSS allowed as qualified educational/train-
ing activities under welfare reform. The New York State Welfare Reform Act of 1997 requires each county in New York to
develop an employment plan. The River Valley County
employment plan outlines client "targets" and work activities
that recipients are obligated to meet and strives to move as
many clients as possible into the workforce. The Plan

> is designed to address the needs of temporary assis-
> tance recipients by providing work activities and sup-
> portive services to prepare these individuals to
> compete in the labor market, while being responsive
> to the needs of these individuals and *allowing them
> to make decisions to the extent permitted by available
> resources and time constraints* [emphasis, mine].
> (River Valley County Department of Social Services
> 1999: 1)

In other words, poor people receive training leading to
employment in jobs that the county has targeted, and it is
questionable as to whether women even want the kind of
training they are offered.

The proliferation of a high-tech sector does not serve the
needs of the poorer residents in Laneville who are unprepared
to work in this sector, although they could be trained to do so.
Whereas emphasis on developing a technology-based industry
in the county has relieved some of the pressures of employment
loss from Zytron's downsizing, poor women are rarely trained
to participate in this sector. Instead, the county focuses on

shaping a labor force suitable primarily for the service sector, keeping many women in an economic bind. Their work opportunities are influenced by the need for low-wage workers, which Sassen (1996) cautiously notes is necessary for the economic growth of an area as part of its infrastructure. Ultimately, those low-wage workers are found in the population of women on welfare, and for battered Black women whose occupational choices are already circumscribed, they are manipulated into participating in predetermined sectors under threat of losing benefits.

River Valley County has an integrated strategy to maximize poor people's participation into the workforce. Having translated the attachment to work concept into a program called River Valley Works, employment counseling and training for anyone who is unemployed is available. The program is a collaborative effort that includes the River Valley County Department of Social Services, the Department of Labor, the Private Industry Council (PIC), the Chamber of Commerce, the Board of Cooperative Educational Services (BOCES), Vocational and Educational Services for Individuals with Disabilities (VESID), the American Association of Retired Persons (AARP), and the River Valley County Economic Development Corporation. While some of these organizations seek to develop the economic base of River Valley, others actually work to mold the labor force to meet the low-wage labor needs of service businesses drawn to the area.

Of course, on the surface, this appears rational and makes good sense because it represents employment opportunities. However, it can also be viewed as an arrangement that facilitates labor force regulation in terms of generating employees for certain sectors and cheapening labor costs by saturating particular sectors with workers. These are the very factors that Ranney (1999) suggests do, in fact, regulate labor markets leading to increased profits, noting that, "economic and government institutions facilitate and intensify competition among workers toward cheapening labor power" (51), which has the potential effect of sustaining poverty, since wages are depressed.

❧

Directives toward work begin when a person applies for Social Services; they are immediately sent to the Department of Labor (DOL) for an orientation with the hope that a job will be found through DOL even before the RVCDSS application is processed. Lori, a supervisor at the Department of Labor, described the program as follows:

> Every day there is an orientation for people who have applied [for social services] from 9:30 a.m. to 10:30 a.m. By doing this, we can move the mindset [of applicants] immediately toward getting a job. If you become a recipient, you are assessed to whether or not you are employable. A highly skilled person can be sent to the Job Club, which is a program operated by the Department of Labor. At the Department of Labor, a TANF or Safety Net recipient can utilize the Resource Room, [where one can learn how to compose a resume or make calls for job listings] which is open from 9:00 a.m. to 4:30 p.m. or receive computer literacy courses. Employer representatives come to DOL to recruit potential employees from the pool of unemployed persons. The DOL oversees a three-pronged Welfare-To-Work Program for TANF and Safety Net recipients: A job club, a training program, and a mentoring program.

The Job Club offers a two-week program helping recipients establish personal goals.[5] The room in which Job Club participants meet has a full-length mirror in it with a sign that reads: "Would you hire you?" This self-assessment is the first step in getting recipients to reinvent themselves in accordance with market imperatives and to socialize them into having a demeanor considered "employable."[6] The program attempts to amend widely circulating perceptions about poor people's human capital deficits by transforming program participants into work-ready persons.

Training and job readiness programs offered by the Department of Labor, Board of Cooperative Educational Services (BOCES), and the Private Industry Council are linked to the private sector through the efforts of the River Valley County Department of Social Services. Private sector needs have been the linchpin around which training and skills building of the social service population has been organized, which the Commissioner of RVCDSS acknowledged:

> They [corporations] didn't trust us, and they saw us and the Department of Labor as having quotas to fill. We wanted to develop that trust with business. . . . I told them I have over a million dollars in training monies. What training are you going to need in the next 5 years for people that are in your business? Do you want keyboarding skills? Give us something we can put our teeth into.

The Commissioner indicated that RVCDSS tailors training to satisfy business interests, and during the time I was in River Valley County, a major corporation was lured to the county with tax incentives and the promise of a low-wage labor supply:

> Well a clothing company came forth and said we need "X" amount of fork-lift operators. So BOCES set up a training program with money, so that if a client comes in and says, I don't know what I want to do and they have driving abilities, we know that if you take this course we're going to have 50 openings at this company.

By hiring welfare recipients, corporations qualify for tax credits, specifically the Work Opportunity Tax Credit (WOTC), which allows a one-time federal credit of $2,400. Then there is the Welfare-to-Work Tax Credit (W2W), which provides a federal tax credit of up to $8,500 over a 2-year period for companies that hire "long-term" recipients of public assistance (New

York State Department of Labor 1998). While these credits serve as an incentive for employers to hire poor people and those with low or nonexistent skills, one critic of the wage subsidy and tax credits has raised several important concerns (Holzer 1999). First among them are, does subsidized employment stigmatize people so as to deflect their participation? Second, do employers taking the subsidy create new jobs or does the subsidy allow employers to get a break on people they would have hired anyway?

Economic restructuring and the expanding service sector drives workforce development, and the poor can be used to fill labor needs. They can be drawn from the TANF and Safety Net population and be made to work. This means female labor comes cheap. Also of concern is how in this process the desires of recipients are pushed aside, and, secondly, how welfare recipients, Black women in particular, are "tracked" into low-skill, low-wage jobs that will rarely allow them to escape the shackles of poverty.

The Department of Social Services acts in the manner of a recruiter on behalf of the private sector's interests, since applicants are prescreened and trained with little regard for self-determination. They are trained in demand occupations—jobs identified by government and business officials as growth areas (Boo 2004). In Sherita's case, the training program she was in had little to do with her actual interests nor her capabilities. Sherita had worked 20 years as an administrative assistant and was employed for a short time at Zytron. As a single woman, she was only eligible for Safety Net funding, the state-sponsored program for single adults. Sherita had work experience coupled with a good employment history and a strong sense of what she wanted to do with her life: she wanted to attend social work school and believed that this could be accomplished by taking classes at River Valley County Community College. No effort was made to help her secure employment in a field in which she had expertise, nor was any effort made to support her educational goals. Instead she attended training in a field in which she actually had little interest, as a certified nursing assistant, to maintain her eligibility for assistance. Although the certificate she earned led to employment, it was not full time, and it was mismatched in terms of the job she actually secured:

> I went and got training as a certified nursing assistant (CNA). What I really want to do is go to River Valley County Community College and work toward getting a degree in social work or human services. But they [RVCDSS] won't let me do that. So I go and finish the training. I get a job at the Home for the Aged. But they tell me my CNA training is not applicable. I have to get retrained as a Personal Care Assistant. When am I going to be able to do that?

Although Sherita became employed as a result of the training, her continued employment was contingent upon her receiving yet another certificate. Because she did not have the time to get a different certificate *and* work enough hours to meet the required number of work hours, over the course of 8 months Sherita switched jobs three times, in an attempt to render relevant the certificate she had earned. Like Leslie and Gina, she made no more than $8 per hour, and, assuming she worked 35 hours every week, which she never did, she earned less than $280 a week. If she did, Sherita's gross salary would have been $14,560 per year, approximately $9,706 after taxes. If this *had* been the case, her income would have exceeded the maximum allowable amount to receive Safety Net funding. But even making about $8,000, she still earned too much, and her benefits were reduced.

I asked the Commissioner of Social Services about the apparent disparity between recipients' desire to receive training based on their personal educational and employment goals and the federal and state goal of moving people to work. He leaned forward and said: "Look, if a person wants to be a hairdresser but the employment demand is for data entry clerks, then that's the training we will give them. We are not going to train people to do jobs that are not available." In other words, people are only trained for jobs that dovetail with the labor needs of the sector driving River Valley's economy, the service sector. There are two aspects to the service economy. One requires credentialing, such as being a certified nursing assistant. The other does not, such as working in a fast-food restaurant. But either way, both require an austere revision of personal goals and skills; both are increasingly competitive (Newman 1999), and both offer little, if any, mobility.

The Violence of Work and Training Programs

Let me restate how important it is to examine the effects of physical violence on women who utilize welfare in light of evidence showing that male abusers undermine women's efforts to leave battering relationships and achieve economic autonomy. Yet the violence/poverty interface takes on increasingly complicated contours in light of local economies and trends that reify the service sector. Through the confluence of several issues Black women who are battered and on welfare experience intense regulation and restrictions on their options. Their options are restricted because of occupational limitations, circumscribed educational opportunities, the extenuating forces of a globalized economy and neoliberal policies. These factors are shuffled on the asymmetries of race and gender, pushing women toward particular occupations by restricting their access to others. Inadvertently or purposefully these restrictions pull on racial stereotypes vis-à-vis occupational segmentation. Policy directives requiring women to participate in racialized work and paying low wages spin an abusive web that reduces economic mobility and produces fear. Fear spins out from being trapped in low-wage work because of constraints on economic survival, and because of the employment options that come with service sector employment. Often low-wage service employment is organized as shift work. For battered women shift work at night increases their sense of vulnerability. Renzetti and Maier (1999) and Websdale (2001) in their respective work on battered women have found that fear of public space defines some women's mobility because they experience a heightened sense of danger as potential targets of their former batterers.

More conservative estimates of neoliberal strategies and the magic of the marketplace report success for those who have left welfare and become employed. But others argue that hiring practices were in fact more beneficial for Whites than Blacks. Even though some conservative reports show that Blacks have had higher reemployment rates than Whites (see for example National Center for Policy Analysis 2002), it has been pointed out that there are different demands to hire recipients by both *race and type* of establishment hiring (Holzer and Stoll 2000). Further, higher employment rates across racial groups does not equate with decreased poverty or hardship.

A second area where racial differentiation in welfare reform policy programs comes into play has to do with accessing education. Under PRWORA, states may count education as a work activity for 20% of their caseload. But, this also means that 80% of a state's recipients are not allowed to count education toward meeting their work goal. Who is allowed to be part of that 20% is left up to, in large measure, the caseworkers who are more likely to offer this opportunity to White women than they are to Black women. Gooden (1998, 1999) notes that there is race-based disparity in the dispensation of information with regard to welfare reform and the incentives to assist women. For example, she found that caseworkers were more likely to encourage and support White than Black women to pursue a college education rather than training. This point comes into sharper focus in the next chapter, but on the surface it certainly illustrates differential treatment by race and is exemplified by the fact that Black women, like Sherita and Leslie, were almost harassed into becoming attached to work, whereas Lorraine, a White woman was not.

Shifts in the global economy, particularly deindustrialization and worker dislocation, have reverberated across the United States diluting employment opportunities that pay a living wage. Loss of industry has wrought havoc in people's lives with few job protections. Job loss in the manufacturing sector alongside the rise of highly skilled occupations has widened the gulf between low and high-income workers with the former being sequestered as a contingent workforce (or what Marx called, "the reserve army of labor"). Concomitantly, the growth of the service sector has generated a need for workers with low-skills who receive inadequate wages and experience insecure employment. Neoliberal solutions that promote reduction of social programs in favor of economic growth view the marketplace as a magic wand, when in reality it is not. Instead it grates up against a host of issues, including who should work and who should not, and extends to attitudes about maternalism, and the class and racial dynamic of who has the capacity to mother. Welfare reform, in addition to ideas about participating in the wage labor force for too little money also aggravates the need for and access to child care and day care.

6

The Theater of Maternal and Child-care Politics

It took two months for Iliana and I to finally meet because, when one of the advocates suggested that I talk with her about her experiences with social services, she was in the last trimester of a difficult pregnancy. I wanted to speak with her because I had been told that her interactions with social services were remarkable in the unyielding manner in which she was pressured to meet the work requirements for her TANF assistance and because of the lack of information she received about the child-care exemptions within the new welfare law. Iliana was often too tired to see me or had an appointment with her caseworker that interfered with our ability to meet.

As an Afro-Latina, Iliana's story illustrates the longstanding role that the state plays in poor Black women's mothering. In other words, historically the state has organized poor, single Black women's ability to mother by forcing them to work through exclusion from public assistance, and now it actively erects barriers to poor, single Black women's mothering by forcing them to work and making their receipt of public assistance tied to work obligations. In this chapter Iliana's story is juxtaposed against that of Susan and Josie, two White women, whose mothering was viewed differentially than hers in relationship to welfare reform mandates.

Iliana was born in the Dominican Republic, where she graduated from high school and attended one year of college.

At age 18, shortly after she began college, her mother died, and she came to the United States to live with her aunt. While in the United States, Iliana met Raphael, the father of her two oldest children, Margie who is 8 and Ricky who is 2. After the birth of her first child, Iliana was primarily a stay-at-home mom, and Raphael worked seasonally doing construction work. When his jobs ended, the family applied for Social Services to counter the financial insecurity brought about by the loss of Raphael's income. His recurring job crisis placed the family in the category of welfare cyclers; those who use social services off and on as a strategy to address the lack of resources. Although she did not say much about Raphael, Iliana did tell me he was abusive and that she had left him.

Iliana obtained welfare on a more long-term basis when she came to the shelter after fleeing from Raphael. At the time of our meeting Iliana received cash assistance, food stamps, and Medicaid. Through the efforts of Angel House advocates, Iliana was able to secure stable housing in the shelter's federally subsidized housing unit for battered women. Since leaving Raphael, she met and has been in a relationship with Tony, the father of her newborn, Rayza—who was just 1 month old when we finally got together.

We began our discussion by talking about the changes in welfare policy. Iliana told me that she was directed to participate in a job-training program to become a Certified Nursing Assistance (CNA). At first she said she didn't mind having been trained as a CNA at BOCES, "because I hoped it would lead me to being employed. I like to work." I found this odd, because no one I met liked being a CNA, but said nothing. Ultimately Iliana became employed as a CNA. Later in the conversation Iliana shared with me that she really did not like being a certified nursing assistant and had hoped for a career in the tourist industry. Unfortunately the training options at BOCES did not include anything related to tourism, although it is a growing industry in Laneville and in the rest of River Valley, as discussed in the previous chapter. This illustrates how recipients' desire to enter particular careers were undermined, ignored, or channeled into certain occupational directions.

But nonetheless, the fact that Iliana wanted to work—like many of the other women I met—made her an ideal TANF recipient. She was compliant with welfare reform's goal . . . except for one thing . . . now with the new baby she was eager to stay home, as she had done with her other two children. She did not feel the baby would be ready to be with a babysitter by 3 months of age.

Before giving birth to Rayza, Iliana enrolled in the CNA training program, learned new skills, and did all that she was told to do by her caseworker. From October through December of 1998 Iliana attended the training, during which time she continued to receive benefits. As a TANF recipient Iliana also received child care assistance from RVCDSS, which under the new law is actually not guaranteed. Under the old program AFDC, states were obligated to provide child care to cash assistance recipients who needed it in order to work or participate in education or training. Under the new law, states do not have an affirmative duty under federal law to subsidize child care to families receiving TANF. However, states are free to maintain that duty under state law to provide assistance, in whole or in part for the cost of child care, but they are not obligated to do so, making Iliana fortunate.

Although she had a grueling schedule, initially her child-care arrangements worked out quite well. Iliana had everything timed to perfection. She arose at 5:30 a.m. and got the children ready to leave by 6:30 a.m. Since she did not have a car, Iliana walked Ricky to the babysitter's house and then walked with Margie to wait for the school bus near the training program site. Her classes for the certificate program began at 8:00 a.m. and lasted until 12:30 p.m.

Welfare reform mandates became more challenging for Iliana; specifically the requirement that one must be engaged in work-related activities for 35 hours per week. The training Iliana attended was 4.5 hours per day or 22.5 hours per week. Shortly after beginning the training program, Iliana received a letter from RVCDSS stating that she had to report to work at a

Food Pantry for community residents. She was told that in order to make up the 12.5 hour difference she had to participate in a workfare program to work off her cash grant. Iliana made sandwiches each day from 12:30 p.m. to 3:00 p.m. Then she had to pick up the youngest child from the baby-sitter and get back to the bus stop to meet Margie. They all walked home, rain or shine, snow or hail. Then something unexpected happened. According to Iliana, "in the first month of the training program, I discovered I was pregnant. I did not plan to get pregnant a third time." Iliana's caseworker questioned her concerning why she continued to have children when she couldn't afford them. Surprised at the underlying implication of the question—that all women on welfare do is have children, Iliana defended herself saying: "I was on the pill. But I had gotten the flu and was given antibiotics. The antibiotics made the pill not work. The people at social services asked me why I keep having children, but things happen . . ." Iliana's explanation did not seem to hold any weight with the caseworker, and Iliana reported that it seemed like the woman did not believe her. Of course the larger issue is that reproduction is not the business of the state but, through policy, as we saw in chapter 2, the state invites itself to weigh in on poor, single Black women's reproductive lives.

In spite of her pregnancy, Iliana remained committed to meeting the mandates. That meant she did not miss school, work, or her community work experience program placement at the Food Pantry or she risked being sanctioned by RVCDSS. Iliana was determined to finish the CNA program and did so in December 1998. Although she was 3 months pregnant, she quickly secured a position at a nursing home working the 7:00 a.m. to 2:00 p.m. shift. The job was only part time, about 28 hours per week, but as soon as she started working, Iliana's cash grant was reduced.

> They didn't want to give me cash because I was making $8.25 an hour. I worked 28–30 hours a week. . . . I still had to go to the Food Pantry. They were trying to make me go because I still needed help

(assistance). They sent me a letter saying I had to be there from 8:30 to 2:00. But I worked from 7:00 to 2:00. I called them and said, 'this conflicts with my work schedule. I have to be at work by 7:00 a.m.' They told me I had to work on my day off. I told them, I have a hard job, I lift people, and I'm pregnant. On my day off I should relax. I didn't want to have a sick baby.

Because Iliana's work hours changed from week to week, and her hours were reported to the River Valley County Department of Social Services, she said she received letters indicating that her food stamp allotment had changed. These letters came almost weekly. For example the weeks she worked 28 hours, Iliana received fewer food stamps, and the weeks she worked less than 28 hours she received more in food stamps. The slightly higher income from working the full 28 hours did not cancel out her need for food stamps. When Iliana worked more hours, the difference in her paycheck was not enough to cover the cost of food when her food stamps were reduced because now she also incurred additional expenses such as transportation costs. Sometimes Iliana had to go to the food pantry where she was assigned to get food for the family.

During her 8th month of pregnancy, while she was still working, Iliana was placed on bed rest for the remainder of her pregnancy. Being home meant that she no longer needed to take her youngest child to day care, but it also meant she lost her child-care slot, and thus the subsidy, because the woman took in another child. She said changes in welfare affected her in this way:

. . . before you could stay home with your children for one year. But now it's only for 3 months. I just found that out when I had the baby. I know I have to work and I don't mind that but they don't give me enough time. . . . I don't know where I will find another baby-sitter. Who will watch the children so early so that I can get to work by 7:00 a.m. in the morning?

I asked Iliana about relying on relatives to help her out with her child-care needs, and she pointed out that the new-born's grandmother is not the grandmother of her other two children. Therefore, she cannot depend on her to watch all three of them. At any rate, she really wants to stay home.

᷒ꙮ

Iliana's situation reveals several issues about welfare reform. First it dismisses her interest in staying home to raise her chil-dren, an indication of the long-standing role of the state in manipulating poor Black women and women of color's mother-ing. Second, her circumstances demonstrate the relationship between work and child care; specifically in terms of the access to and quality of child care that one might have to accept when one is mandated to work. For example, since Iliana wanted to stay home, she might have worked a later shift, from 9:00 p.m. to 4:00 a.m. When I raised this possibility Iliana told me that she would never see her children if she worked the "third shift." She also thought it was highly improbable that an appropriate child-care provider could be found who was will-ing to work at those hours. This in turn raised the issue of the quality of child care. What type of quality was she expected to accept in order to meet her work obligations? Finally, Iliana's situation embodies the problem of the lack of information given to some women about working and child care. According to federal law, states cannot sanction single parents caring for chil-dren *under 6 years* of age for failure to meet work requirements if the parent can demonstrate an inability to find appropriate child care, but Iliana was unaware of this protection. She was under the impression that she had to go to work, even though her child would only be 3 months old when she returned, and even if she did not have child care. Iliana felt pressured to con-form to welfare reform mandates, because she received a bar-rage of letters from social services. Intimidated by the correspondence, Iliana thought that she would lose all of her benefits. "They must have been thinking of me everyday at Social Services. I would get a letter every week. I do what they want [get training and get a job] and the letters still keep coming. They still take stuff away from me."

The letters itemized what Iliana was expected to do to keep her benefits and reported changes in her food stamp allotment based on her fluctuating income. Each time she received a letter, she went to RVCDSS to meet with her caseworker. Iliana's days were often determined by social services and the frequency with which she was expected to respond to them interfered with her ability to spend quality time with her children.

The degree to which she worried was so stressful that she reported being sleep deprived staying awake and trying to come to terms with the fact that although she wanted to stay home that desire would probably not be realized. Then she lay awake worried about how to resolve her child-care dilemma, since she lost her slot. Near the end of our interview, Iliana said that what they expected of her was demanding. "They don't see it's so hard for me." Having to respond to the gatekeepers of her survival was daunting.

Denying women like Iliana the choice to stay home and raise their children represents a shift in how the United States has viewed mothering. Historically, patriarchal ideology in the United States has anticipated that mothers would devote themselves to unpaid domestic work, rather than wage labor. Commitment to motherhood was viewed as a core component of a healthy society and in fact enjoyed support from states beginning around 1911 with the advent of Mothers' Pensions. Pensions helped support the goal of mothers cultivating good citizens, who were compelled to extend the moral values and social caring of the home to the larger community (Skocpol 1992). The very idea of women working and leaving their children was viewed as the downfall of the familial unit (Zylan 2000).

Of course this perspective of mothering was, and continues to be, embedded in race and class politics, for in 1911 not all mothers were entitled to the support allowing them to stay at home to nurture their children. By excluding some women from receiving Mothers' Pensions to facilitate the role of maternal care, according to Abramovitz (1996) the state mediated the demands of partriarchal capitalism by urging women to provide two functions (1) to remain home in order to reproduce and maintain the labor force; and (2) to do traditionally female low-wage work in the paid labor force. The racial translation of this ideology meant that mostly Black, women of color, single, and immigrant women worked, while primarily White women stayed home.

From the early 1900s to the mid-twentieth century,[1] support was awarded only to White widowed mothers because they were considered ideal for domestic labor. They were the ones who met societal standards of moral fitness and worthiness. In the mid-1930s the policy translation of this ideology in terms of welfare programs was the provision of aid to support the domestic labor of White women who were or had been attached to men. Following support for this version of maternalism in the form of Mother's Pensions, in the 1900s Aid to Dependent Children became the program through which government support was available to women with children. Funds were provided to states from the federal government to establish programs for children who received the federal grant. The program Aid to Dependent Children (ADC) was designed to grant benefits to the children of nonworking mothers who were widowed or estranged from their husbands. Low-income Black women were discouraged from mothering and received little federal support through ADC. We must pause and also remember that discouraging Black women and other women of color from mothering had been imported through the eugenics movement at the turn of the twentieth century and later sterilization laws. Both have attempted to control the reproduction of the "unfit," which often meant controlling Black women's fecundity (Thomas 1998).

Essentially from 1935 forward, there was active financial support for White widowed mothers to engage in maternal care. Denied access to Aid to Dependent Children meant that

Black, single, immigrant and women of color mothers were unable to care for their children at home because they were forced to work. This, in the face of popular belief that if a woman worked, she reduced her own chances of becoming married. Thus working women interrupted the sanctity and maintenance of the male-headed household. So classified by their racial, immigrant and/or marital status (Quadagno 1994; Handler 1995), specific groups of women were forced into the wage labor market because their productive labor was necessary for a growing industrial society while simultaneously being chastized for doing so.

As pointed out in chapter 2, when ADC became AFDC in 1962, Black women were able to access support. Policymakers were riled at the demographic shift in welfare recipients, bemoaning Black female heads of households. Consequently there was one brief ideological interruption in Black women's historical obligation to work. That was when the Nixon administration attempted to mold impoverished Black families into the White nuclear family model by providing assistance to Black men, so they could assert their role as heads of households.

Contemporarily, the politics of mothering for poor and working-class women of color on public assistance have been restaged based on early to mid-twentieth-century norms of harnessing their productive labor. This time however, instead of using acts of omission, i.e. excluding Black and women of color from support to force them into the labor market, welfare reform policies actively penalize women by withholding assistance if they do not become attached to work, to achieve the same goal. In linking receipt of assistance to maternal employment—leaving the home—welfare policy interferes with poor women's mothering choices and restricts their freedom to move between home and the market. The ideology of mothering continues to shape-shift around race and is startling when one looks at how within class, there is differential treatment of White versus Black women on Temporary Assistance for Needy Families. As opposed to working, White women receive more support for their mothering choices than Black women do, evidenced by Susan's story.

Susan, a White Battered Woman on Welfare

Susan is a 36-year-old White woman with a set of 8-year-old twins and four other children. Susan was actually the first woman I ever interviewed, and of all the women I had interviewed had one of the most complicated linkages with institutions. Susan had been engaged with Social Services, Child Protective Services, the court system, and law enforcement agencies, among others. Susan was in fact the only person I met who most closely resembles the public's view of a "welfare mother," except that she was White. She was young, had lots of children, and had collected welfare for most of her adult life, rarely holding a job. Eager to share her story with someone, Susan told me that she left the state in which she lived to get away from her abuser.

Susan was illiterate. Rather, she was functionally literate in that she could sign her name and read some words, but filling out job applications was trial by fire for her. This situation made Susan the only woman interviewed who needed to take remedial courses. She was a former alcoholic and regularly attended Alcoholics Anonymous meetings. Her sponsor in fact was the one who helped her escape the battering relationship she was in. Despite her limitations, Susan's case at Angel House was not terribly complicated. She was able to stabilize her life relatively quickly, for like other White women, Susan easily found a place to live in a town nearby Laneville. Although it was a trailer home, she secured it in less than 2 months after arriving at the shelter. As will be discussed in the next chapter, this was quite different than most of the Black women and women of color who were often *at* the 3-month mark when they found housing. But in addition to being able to use the privilege of Whiteness to locate housing relatively quickly and outside of the city, the other thing that was remarkable about Susan was that she did not receive the same kind of push to work as Iliana or Leslie did. Susan's children were 8 years old, much older than either Iliana or Leslie's newborns, and while she was told by her caseworker that she would have to find work, the sense that she would be sanctioned or cut off from receiving assistance did not flood her life in the way that it did for Iliana or Leslie. Ultimately, Susan found a job at a fast-food restaurant, the same type of low-wage, contingent job other women found. But it seemed to be within her own timeframe because no caseworker made her feel vulnerable. This poor White women was more successful in entering the job market.

While Black women experience a multitude of hardships and demands within the environment of welfare reform, White battered women receive less abrasive treatment from case-workers toward their mothering and work obligations making the theater of maternal politics for poor women multiply refer-ential. In other words while welfare reform and work man-dates seem to apply broadly to poor single women, it really is directed to both single Black mothers who are presumed to need governmental prodding to go to work and to White mothers who receive comparatively beneficent treatment within a system that is generally alienating.

The new welfare law "presumes that if a caregiver is unmar-ried, then paid child-care is preferable to having her stay home and care for her own children" (Mink 1998: 108). This emphasis on employment immediately raised issues of child and day care with regard to women's ability to access care, its affordability and in terms of the quality of care; in relation to the conflict work raises for women who want to stay home; and how information about work obligation and child care is disseminated. All of these factors were problems Iliana faced, as she was being directed to training programs and low wage labor participation.

Since the 1940s lubricating the possibility of women working has been day care and child care, because lack of these resources are a major hindrance to poor mothers' labor force participation (Kimmel 1994). Then, as now, effectively incorporating women into the labor force is hampered by the needs for child and day care, a concern that was addressed by the nation's experiment with supporting child and day care through the Lanham Act in 1941 (Zylan 2000). Shortly after WWII, however, Congress terminated support for day-care funding. The idea of a national experiment in day care was not reissued until 1962, but it was not supported. It is odd that despite the fact that although the nation forced women to work or be engaged in work-related activity through PRWORA in 1996, there was no sound national day care or child care proposal.

Child care stands in the forefront of anxiety about welfare reform because the mandate to work does not come with assurances of a living wage. Single-parent families, like Iliana's, are likely to pay more for child care than are two-parent families. As a percentage of earnings, single parents pay approximately 16% of their salaries. When earnings are low, the level of child-care expense could affect whether a family is able to 'make it'. Among poor families on welfare, they pay about 18% of their earnings on child-care. For families who earn less than the official poverty level, child-care expenses can range from 23–34% of their earnings (Giannarelli and Barismantov 2000).

Iliana was unsure what type of child-care arrangements she would be able to secure at the time we met, since she had lost her provider when she was put on bed rest. There was a woman in the neighborhood who might be willing to help her out, she said. But informal child-care arrangements are frequently arranged with people who do not view the arrangement as primary. The providers, mostly low-income mothers tend to have responsibilities and obligations to people other than the child in need of care (Henly 1998). Their lack of commitment threatens the stability of the arrangement and places mothers at risk in terms of ongoing employment. This is why many women try to use relatives for child care, since it is presumed there will be more flexibility. But even that strategy comes with limitations when families are constituted in different ways. For example, Iliana thought she might be able to get Tony's mother to commit to watching her new granddaughter, Rayza. But she would probably not care for Iliana's other two children, Margie and Ricky, who had a different father. Iliana was unable to utilize the child and day-care resources made available by the River Valley County Department of Social Services.

Child care in River Valley County is limited and has been for the last 6 years. The need for it has been partially resolved by increasing the number of day-care centers, but demand continues to exceed supply. RVCDSS subsidizes day care for mothers on public assistance and for low-income families, but suitable caregivers are still extremely difficult to find. In 1999 the county budgeted over $2 million for child-care assistance and subsidies. Approximately 1,000 children of public assistance recipients receive day-care subsidies from RVCDSS. Just over 600 people from low-income families also receive help from RVCDSS, but there is a long waiting list. The Commissioner of RVCDSS informed me that the Department's own research found that the waiting list was long because women who do not need child care immediately (because they are still pregnant) are prematurely signing up to ensure a spot at the time the child turns 3 months old. One might surmise, however, if women are signing up prematurely, then clearly they are anticipating a shortage.

Child- and day-care accessibility and shortages speak to the mandate that women work. What they do not speak to is the issue of how, among women who feel bound to fulfill their role as mothers, some get to choose and are supported in their parenting options, while others like Iliana, simply have little choice, or else they risk losing their economic support. Kalil, Schweingruber, Daniel-Echols, and Breen (2000) note in their study on mothers who work and receive welfare, child care is a conflicted issue for women. Mothers experience conflict because by working (or participating in training programs), they are required to spend too many hours away from their children and are reluctant to let unknown child-care providers be responsible for their children. The expectation that women must work or be engaged in work-related activities in order to remain eligible for TANF does not take into account either maternal feelings or women's desire to find a child care provider with whom they are comfortable. Caseworkers are often insensitive to women's concerns about their child-care options. Child-care decisions create a clash between a woman's ability to work and her sense of what makes her a good mother. Women should not be forced to parent in ways that are contrary to their own value systems. By that I mean that if their value systems include working, they should be able to do so. If their value systems include being stay-at-home moms, which is what Iliana wanted to do, then they should be able to enjoy that right.

The third issue that Iliana's story raises is the lack of information about her obligation to meet work mandates in the absence of child care. Although mothers cannot be sanctioned for not complying with work requirements if they are unable to access appropriate child care, many worry that they will be sanctioned. By law, however, caseworkers are required to inform parents that they cannot be penalized for that reason. Yet, some are not told of their child-care rights, as was the case with Iliana. In her effort to meet mandates, Iliana went to BOCES for training and went daily to the food pantry to work off her grant. Although she worked hard, the demands of reform left Iliana feeling tired and fragmented.

Comparing Illiana's situation to that of Josie, a young White woman, we see how the state's support of mothering is biased, and how race colludes with the delivery of different levels of information about child-care and work mandates, reflecting different maternal expectations. Josie's experience reveals quite a departure in caseworker management for a client who is supposed to be engaged in work or work-related activity. The support Josie received from her caseworker was sympathetic; congruent with the type of support many White women received, an indication of just whom some caseworkers thought should be able to stay home with their children.

Josie is a White woman who is 25. She has a daughter, Shaneva, by Luke. When Josie met Luke, a 27-year-old, charming Black man who was a file clerk, his charm "got to her," and she fell in love. Within one month of their dating, Josie discovered she was pregnant. The two set about saving for their wedding, but during that year Luke became abusive. Originally from the South, Josie moved to River Valley County at age 17. She remembers that her father used to beat her mother who nonetheless had five children by him. After the family moved to River Valley and her father abandoned them, Josie's mother was forced to go on welfare.

Constantly planning for her future life in much the same way as Leslie, whose situation is one of the case studies detailed in chapter 4, Josie wants her daughter to see her as a success and wants to raise her child with the love and affection she felt she never got. Josie never tires of Shaneva and holds her constantly, even when Shaneva is sleeping. The circumstance of violence and no income of course meant that Josie had to use social services to deal with the changes in her life. She needed a place to stay and a source of income. Josie was no stranger to social services and had been on public assistance since she was 19 because she wanted to live on her own and get away from her family. Her social service conundrum had to do with whether she should use the Child Support Collection Unit to receive $100 per week from Luke, or not. Each state is required to enforce child support systems in order for that state to meet federal standards. Families that apply for TANF must cooperate with the child support program. Under the old rules, the first $50 per month of child support collected was passed through to families who were receiving AFDC. Under the new rules, states collect child support, but the mothers do not receive any money. The state keeps 100% of the child support payments as reimbursement for TANF benefits paid. It has been astutely pointed out that the amount of child support payments that is used to reimburse the state for TANF benefits has no effect on the recipients' welfare time limits (Gordon 2001). It stands to reason that if the state has been reimbursed for part of its benefit disbursement through child support, then during that time the clock should be stopped, so there are no charges against a recipient's time limit.

But the Family Violence Option (FVO) gives women latitude, so they do not have to file for child support payment because if they were to contact their children's fathers, retaliation might be possible. Because of Luke's behavior, Josie filed a restraining order against him, unknowingly leveraging the possibility that she would be exempt from having to collect child support. When Josie and I spoke prior to her going to RVCDSS, she had no idea about the FVO exemption. She did not know what it was. After seeing a caseworker, she decided to forego collecting child support from Luke because the caseworker with whom she met at RVCDSS willingly provided her with information to help in her decision-making process. This included being told about the how the domestic violence liaison could sign a child support waiver.

With one exception, Clemmie, no other Black woman received information about the Family Violence Option. Yet White women were provided with such information, with greater regularity. Lauren, a shelter advocate who had accompanied Josie to her social services appointment noticed the differential treatment between White and Black clients. Lauren had also accompanied a young Black woman to see the same caseworker Josie had met with and was appalled at how differently each woman was treated. She said:

> Ms. Harris provided Josie with all of the necessary information she needed to get through the social service maze. She explained to her how the requirements could be used to help her achieve her goals. She told her that if she wanted to go to school, RVCDSS would pay for her transportation to class and provide her with day care. Ms. Harris told her that they could even figure out a way to let her go to school for two years if she wanted and that she would not have to work, since Shaneva was less than 1 year old. Ms. Harris was so helpful. They needed Luke's license

number, which Josie did not have. Ms. Harris said, 'I'll call for you.' In determining the benefits, Ms. Harris called Yvonne Genesee to see if Josie could secure a waiver for child support. When Josie filled out some boxes on her application incorrectly, Ms. Harris went over it with her and explained what it was she had done incorrectly. It seemed like she reached out to Josie. But that's not right. She didn't do that with Linda, [who is Black] who also had a young child. She was rude and did not even bother to answer questions that we had about Linda's case. If you're going to be a caseworker, you've got to give everybody the same amount of information and care.

Collectively Susan's and Josie's experiences exemplify how mothering is constructed along racial lines and that White mothers are more supported in their maternal options. For example the fact that Susan was *not* aggressively pushed toward working, although she did ultimately work, suggests that maybe she is somehow more appropriate as a mother than as a worker. Ms. Harris's comment that Josie "would not have to work" since Shaneva was less than 1 year old, reflects how *maternal care* is encouraged as a more appropriate choice. When compared to the two Black women, Iliana and Leslie, both of whom received directives to become attached to work, *maternal employment* superceded maternal care.

Expectations of mothering are enacted through class and race, and can be measured in part by examining its staging within the broader "mommy war" debates. This debate centers around the choices, benefits, detriments, and politics of mothers staying at home or working (Crittenden 2002; Lewis and Yoest 1996). The public face of this debate is dominated primarily by White upper-middle-class and professional women. According to the U.S. Census Bureau, 20% of stay at home moms live in households earning $100,000 or more, while 2.3% are in households earning less than $10,000. Among those women who choose to exit their profession in order to mother, there is a badge of honor for having made the sacrifice

of leaving their high-paying jobs (Wallis 2004). Those who opt
to work often lament or praise their dependence on either low-
paid caregivers or certified child-care providers like nannies.
But the discourse of this debate and those who constitute soldiers in the mommy wars are not burdened often enough by a
class and race analysis. Analytical exclusion sustains the theory
and the accepted practice that White women are and should be
the ones who get to "choose" between home or market. Also
by excluding a class and race analysis, poor single mothers and
mothers of color do not have to be accounted for as mothers,
reinforcing the fact that staying home is really not a widely
supported option for them.

What is glossed over is that even within race but across
class, there are tensions about Black women's mothering. For
example Black middle-class women have historically been less
likely to be stay-at-home moms because they have typically
combined mothering and wage labor in greater numbers than
White women. Blending work with family and community obligations, Black women have challenged the barriers that have
interfered with the devotion to and preservation of family and
community. Yet increasingly Black middle-class women have
opted to be stay-at-home mothers, although they are rarely the
subject of the media's mommy-war obsession. Regardless, there
is less enthusiasm about Black women who stay home. Some
Black women professionals, according to the popular media,
who have left the workforce report being "charged" with wast-
ing their education by friends and families (Caviness 2002).
Whereas among White families, stay-at-home moms are traditionally accepted, this is a new trend among Black families.
While White women's status as workers and mothers generates
considerable discussion in the public sphere, whether or not it is
more or less beneficial for Black women or women of color to
work or stay home receives very little media coverage. One
reason is because Black women, regardless of their professional
status, have traditionally participated in the labor force, where
their work obligations are anticipated. There is little fanfare
about their potential conflicts between work and mothering.

Class seems to make little difference in public discussion
about Black women and mothering. Few middle and upper

middle class Black women are represented as part of the debates about maternal choice. And, fewer poor and working poor Black mothers' maternal issues stimuilate public concern. Meanwhile class distinctions lie at the heart of how women's labor is viewed *and* what child care means. For example, elite professional women are often working for emotional fulfillment and may choose to exit the labor force knowing they have the resources to do so. They do not depend on caregivers in the same ways as midrange professional women and low-wage or no-wage mothers do. The latter group of women are often just barely making ends meet, and their reliance on child care is fundamental to their survival. As Flanagan (2004) points out, two women can enter the labor force for every one that has a new job (regardless of the what the pay is), and both drive economic growth in profound ways.

The theater of maternal and child-care politics has different acts, many of which can be framed within the context of class and race. Across class, expectations of mothering are differentially orchestrated, because choices about mothering and child-care needs are supposed to be congruent with what resources one has. The "mommy war" debate takes the nation's temperature around the appropriateness of maternal caregiving—for elite women. Among women who need public assistance the temperature drops; there is little to no debate because the expectation leans toward maternal employment.

We can see more sharply how class differences in maternal expectations are managed by race. Elite White women are most often cast in leading roles in the theater of the "mommy war"—who gets to choose to stay home or not (see Gibbs 2002; Wallis 2004). Within the context of welfare policy mandates, although all poor women are expected to work, the privilege of Whiteness redirects the aggressive focus of maternal employment toward maternal care, as evidenced by how Susan and Josie were not patently pushed toward employment in the same way that Iliana and Leslie were. Iliana and Leslie exemplify how the desire to stay home with their children is not supported in racial terms. Consequently the uneven application of maternal caregiving choices reinforces who is appropriate to care for children and who is not, based on race and class.

7

There's No Place (Like Home)

Due to women's experience with violence, they were forced to leave their homes, having effectively been evicted in order to save their own lives and those of their children. The women who left their abusers and are on welfare need housing assistance in order to set up households. Until they are housed, they are homeless, and one of the first processes initiated after entering the shelter is that of finding a home.

However, locating a place to live is increasingly difficult for poor and low-income people across the United States due to the depletion of affordable housing in cities like Laneville. According to the U.S. Conference on Mayors Task Force on Hunger and Homelessness in 2001,

> Lack of affordable housing leads the list of causes of homelessness identified by the city officials. Other causes cited in order of frequency, include low pay jobs, substance abuse and the lack of needed services, mental illness and the lack of needed services, domestic violence, unemployment, poverty, prison release and changes and cuts in public assistance programs (Prashad 2003, 29–30).

Over the last decade, the number of affordable rental units nationwide has declined. Decreases in housing stock result primarily from rental increases that push existing units out of the affordable range. In Laneville unaffordable housing is linked to the problem of economic decline and the city's subsequent revitalization and gentrification efforts, which deployed aggressive real estate and incentive activities. Deindustrialization has been met with a range of economic and development schemes across the United States in cities that have strategized ways to rebuild not only their economies but also to resurrect the physical space of their communities. Laneville is no different, and like many communities across the country, it is a city where the revival of spatial arrangements, just like the previous spatial arrangements, is influenced by race.

In this chapter, I explore the intersection of Laneville's residential landscape and the city's revitalization efforts, which effectively obstruct women's ability to become successfully housed. In the first part I describe the racialized pattern of housing in Laneville. I came to understand how residential areas were racialized by talking with several community residents and community advocates. One in particular, Juliet, was my "residential guide." Juliet is an African-American community activist in her 50s who has lived in Laneville for 30 years. She opened up her home to me, often allowing me to spend the night. We would leave in the morning and return each evening, each time taking a slightly different route. During our walks she pointed out and commented on Laneville's housing issues. Her sensitivity to the housing needs of battered women on welfare was an important factor in how she understood the state of housing in Laneville, and she expressed disgust when I shared Joanne's story, one of the case studies that follows below, showing one consequence of poverty.

Revitalization efforts and their impact on women who are Black, battered, and on welfare, are also discussed. These efforts preclude them from finding places to live and set the stage for moving them from the "racially designated spaces" they are currently allowed to occupy, to somewhere else. When viewed as intersecting points, we see how local revitalization efforts are a hindrance to affordable housing and yet another example of the structural violence that battered Black women on welfare face.

Race, Violence, and Housing

Early one morning I sat at the dining room table with the shelter staff and in came Diane, a Black woman in her 30s. As she entered, she said, "Where's the paper? I've got to find a place." I gave her my copy, and she sat down examining the real estate section of the Laneville Journal. She marked off two apartment listings with blue pen. I noticed that there were other ads and asked, "Why don't you check out some of these?" pointing to the other listings. She replied: "I can't live there, that's Downtown."

Diane's comment referenced the fact that there was a dividing line, Division Street, that demarcated where Black people lived, and where they did not. Or rather, where they could, and where they could not live. Division Street cuts through Laneville, producing residential arrangements based on race and class. One side of Division Street is the area known as Downtown, which is where primarily middle- and upper-middle-class White residents live. The homes in this area have both front and back acreage, and many of the houses are large Victorian style homes. The status that has been bestowed upon many homes in this area is evidenced by the historic landmark designation for almost every house for a five-block stretch on one street, Fieldstone Street. There are a few rentals in Downtown, and houses cost upwards of $85,000. This is the neighborhood that was out of reach for Black women, like Diane, who were leaving the shelter and setting up independent homes.

On the other side of Division Street is the neighborhood known as Uptown. It is here that most of the women lived and is the section of the city with an "urban," [read Black and Latino], population. While some of the homes are also Victorian, such as those in Downtown, they are in various stages of disrepair and sell for as little as $38,000. Despite the historic significance some houses may have had, not one house in Uptown was designated as an historic landmark.

Juliet lives in Uptown in a home built in 1910, which has been in her family for over half a century. On the side of the block where Juliet's house is located there are eight homes, most of which were built in the early 1900s. Three are owner-occupied, and four have the same absentee landlord who rents out the houses and checks on her properties daily, unlike many landlords. The other is a rooming house that is essentially a drug den.

Variations in properties, private ownership, absentee land-lord rentals, and rooming houses characterize Uptown. In addition, Uptown, unlike Downtown, has several businesses interspersed among the residential dwellings, including an office supply store, small manufacturing companies, and the county jail. Unlike Downtown, Uptown also has concentra-tions of public housing, where poor people, mostly of color, are essentially sequestered. Even along the border between Uptown and Downtown, which is underdeveloped but also under development, I soon discovered that racial restrictions existed when Leslie and I attempted to secure an apartment for her. We passed a beautiful old brick building that had been recently renovated on the border of Downtown. A mixed-use building, it had a street-level business and an apartment upstairs. In the window of the business, a sign indicated that the apartment above was for rent. The two of us Black women—one of whom was pregnant—went in and inquired about the vacancy and were told it was rented. Leslie immedi-ately sensed that the apartment "became" unavailable because of the color of our skin. As we left, I noted the phone number on the sign and later called, putting on my best "White" people's voice and asked if the apartment was available. I was told yes, and that it was a "beautiful duplex apartment with lots of light, renting for $850 a month."

Even though the apartment was available, there was absolutely no way Leslie or any of the other women could have afforded the rent, because a woman receiving assistance from RVCDSS must find an apartment within the parameters of the housing budget she is given. Table 1 below shows the monthly rent allowance from public assistance based on the number of people in the household:

TABLE 1

Public Assistance Monthly Allowance for Shelter with Heat,
Based on Number of People in Household

Number of people	Monthly Allowance
1	$353
2	469
3	579
4	689
5	803
6	886

Source: PA/FS/MA/Monthly Allowances and Income Levels 8/15/96 (revised)

These monthly allowances prohibit women from moving to residences of their choice, which is often in Downtown. This, of course, means that they almost always have to live in Uptown, where the rents are more compatible with housing allowance guidelines. The places women desired to live were financially out-of-reach. Leslie, for example, was given a budget of $347 for an apartment.[1] One listing in the *Laneville Journal*, a "two bedroom," fell within her budget, and we went to see it. Leslie naively hoped the space was bright and airy, but as we neared the street on which the apartment was located, she looked dejected. The apartment was located right next to a building known for drug activity. The buzzer system did not work, and the apartment was on the first floor. Leslie yelled for someone to let us in, and when we entered, disappointment fell over her. The living room was the "first bedroom," located in the front of the house and was less than 7 feet wide. The "second bedroom" was barely a room at 5 feet wide. Small, low windows in both rooms looked out on to a porch, but the absence of protective window bars made Leslie uncomfortable, and she observed that "anybody could break into the apartment," a reasonable concern given the fact that a crack house was next door. The kitchen, the largest room in the apartment, was in the rear and was infested with roaches. Leslie simply looked at me and said, "How can I raise my baby in this?"

Leslie was angry that she was "expected" to live in such a place, in the sense that in the absence of other options, this was what she had to take. Obtaining housing is punctuated by race, given the racial dividing line that cuts Laneville in half. While this is one example of a structured inequality, there were other barriers to housing that lurked in sanctioning, one of the punitive parts of welfare reform, and in the biases that came because women had been victimized.

First, as previously stated, women in shelters have been forcibly evicted from their homes due to violence. Entering the shelter system for battered women makes them homeless and shelter stay limits, set at 90 days, means that finding housing is of the utmost importance. Housing is already a racialized proposition, since women cannot afford to move into neighborhoods of their choice and are relegated to Uptown. Even so, within Uptown, they are most interested in living in private homes and do not want to be concentrated in public housing buildings. Women's choices are limited because of the low rent allocations. But their desire to live in private housing is related to punitive welfare policy. The possibility of case closure, being sanctioned, or having their benefits reduced mean that women can experience the loss of financial support at any time. If they live in a public housing unit, they are unable to negotiate alternative payment plans with their landlord, the Public Housing Authority. Even though the rent is based on a percentage of the income or based on a housing allocation, if a person is sanctioned or has their benefits reduced, then they would still have to come up with the difference. If, on the other hand, they live in privately owned homes, they can conceivably arrange to make rent payments over time instead of once in the beginning of a month, if need be.

Bias against women who experience intimate violence also plays a role in women's housing options as well. When many Black battered women completed rental applications, the contact address was the shelter. Correspondence would be sent to: The woman's name, c/o Angel House, P.O. Box XXX. Everybody knows what Angel House is, and small property owners were not always inclined to rent to women who were formerly battered, fearful that the violence would follow her to their property. Some advocates advised women to only provide the shelter's P.O. Box address and omit the phrase "c/o Angel House" or were instructed not to tell the landlord that they were battered. Of course, there is a paradox in having to leave one's home because of violence and then being unable to secure a home because of violence.

Race, welfare, and violence conspired against women's potential safety in ways that were not often easy to discern. Restricted residential options were not always apparent to the women, because sometimes advocates made calls to determine rental availability on women's behalf. They did not share with them the outcome of conversations that began with "I am calling from Angel House for a client who is in need of housing." Women were not always told that landlords did not want victims of domestic violence living in their units. For Latina women, advocates were often informed that no rentals were available after the realtor had been given a woman's last name. Surnames like Jimenez, Sanchez, etc., were enough to prevent a woman from even seeing an apartment. Some Black women who met with landlords, of course, were never directly told they could not rent an apartment; they were just told the apartment was taken. In the case of battered women, the fact that they were denied an apartment because they were battered was skirted around; the landlord simply might not call her back. So, being a poor woman, battered, and Black meant one never knew precisely what the prevailing reason was for being turned down. Was it because of class, gender, violence, or race? Or was it some combination of all four?

In the final analysis, the value women place on a home is rooted in their desire to be safe. Fitchen (1981), in her work on rural poverty, discusses the dissonance in values between those who are poor and those who are middle class. She suggests that the housing goals differ between the two groups, arguing that poor people accept inexpensive, substandard housing and are willing to compromise between ideal preferences and real prospects. Consequently there is vulnerability in being publicly scrutinized and labeled as lazy, spendthrift, and without ambition as a result of living in poor housing. However, women like Diane and Leslie had little opportunity to "compromise." Since compromise implies agreement by mutual consent, one would be hard-pressed to suggest that these women compromised. Their housing choices were limited a priori as a result of race, violence, and poverty.

Residential segregation by race has been widely documented as a contributing cause of poverty (Massey and Denton 1992), and historical patterns of housing segregation are nowhere near being resolved (see, for example, Goode and Johnson 2003). Housing discrimination is still likely to occur in metropolitan housing markets, according to Turner, et al. (2002), who notes that African Americans receive less favorable treatment by realtors than do Whites. Women knew what they wanted, but their multiple statuses were structural barriers forcing them to shift their housing goals without their consent; instead they shrank their desires to fit into the spaces that were available to them.

Availability of quality housing for women on a TANF budget was very, very limited, as Sara, a White woman with a long history of advocacy in the community on behalf of battered women, made clear. Sara had been attempting to locate an apartment for one of her clients and was frustrated by what was out there for women, remarking: "Some of the places are real shit." To this comment she adds:

> You can't afford to live in anything decent. If a woman comes to me and tells me the address of the place she's going to look at, and I know it's a bad block, I'll tell her. But sometimes they don't have a choice. There's housing, but it's cheap housing. The landlords know what the maximum budget is for each family size on social services. The people who manage the slum building are like loan sharks. The apartment owners rip people off. Like Mr. Johnson—he owns a building where none of the apartments have refrigerators. He also owns an appliance store. So when a woman on social services goes to

his building, she has to buy a refrigerator for the apartment in order for it to be certified. When the woman leaves the apartment, he takes the fridge out of the apartment and brings it to the store, and DSS buys it again. DSS pays for the same fridge over and over.

Here we see that in addition to how the interplay of race and violence limits accessibility, women are also subjected to a series of microtests in order to secure an apartment. In the course of this process, they confront numerous impediments while attempting to set up households. In the next case study, centering on Joanne, the complication of trying to get *into* an apartment even after one has been found, is described.

Joanne is a small, demure Black woman in her 20s with one child and is pregnant with her second. Joanne has lived in Uptown for the past 5 years with her son and her boyfriend, Carl, and she came to the shelter in the fall of 1998, after Carl beat her. Carl returned home one September evening after work and saw Joanne standing in front of their apartment building talking with friends. He was in a foul mood, and when he got out of the cab, he began arguing with Joanne about what, she did not remember. Carl started beating Joanne in the street. The next day Joanne and her son JD came to the shelter. Within a day she was at the River Valley Department of Social Services applying for assistance, and she quickly began her search for an apartment.

In her search Joanne submitted five applications with realtors for apartments in the Downtown area. Joanne wanted to live in Downtown as a strategy to decrease the probability that she would run into Carl. She also wanted to live in a safe place but was rejected by each agency, she believed, because she was Black. Unable to find an apartment in Downtown, Joanne become desperate because all she wanted was to have a home, a quiet, violence-free place to raise JD and the new baby.

Joanne might be described as the ideal TANF recipient—she already had a job working part time in accounts payable at a small company, so mandatory work would not be a problem for her. Her immediate need for social services was due to the loss of Carl's income, and she was unable to afford housing costs on her own.

It took Joanne a full 3 months to find a place to rent, but when she did it was in Uptown, an area she did not think was a good place to raise the children. "It's not really safe . . . but it's all there is," she said. However, this apartment did not have a refrigerator, making it unsuitable for certification by RVCDSS. Without the refrigerator, her move-in date was delayed. Joanne's RVCDSS caseworker told her to get an estimate for the appliance and have it faxed to the office. Once received and approved, RVCDSS would pay for the fridge, have it delivered, and then she could move in.

The search began. Joanne, myself, and Angie, a shelter advocate, went early one morning to get an estimate on a refrigerator. We tried three locations, two of which had refrigerators on the street just outside the entrance of their stores. At the first store, Angie immediately asked for an estimate on the appliance and the salesman said, "no." He was clearly familiar with social services language enough to know that an estimate was connected to welfare. He held up his hand and waved her away saying, "We don't give estimates for welfare . . . they don't buy the new ones. We only have new ones."

Looking down at the floor, Joanne was embarrassed and headed for the front door. Angie attempted to console her by saying "Let's try another place. I saw a place that looks like they may have used appliances." The second shop had no more refrigerators. The third shop, which appeared to be a florist shop had a refrigerator. Angie walked over to a man who looked like he was in charge and asked if they gave estimates. "We don't give estimates no more. Welfare has to call us first and then we'll deliver." Angie pleaded with him to fax the estimate to RVCDSS, but he became exasperated and walked over to an old desk. He opened the top drawer and pulled out a dog-eared piece of paper. Waving the paper in

Angie's face he said, "We did estimates, but then no one showed up to get the appliance. No one comes, and it takes too much time." By now Joanne looked desperate and whispered to me "I can't get the apartment approved without the refrigerator."

That Sunday following our attempt to locate a refrigerator, Joanne looked depressed. She spoke slowly while making chili for the shelter residents, as it was her turn to cook dinner. She told me she was tired and scared because the apartment had not yet been inspected, and she only had 3 days left before she had to leave the shelter. Her emotions fluctuated between being euphoric at having found a place, disappointed because the apartment was not in the neighborhood she wanted to live in, and being depressed that although she found a place, her ability to move in was contingent upon a refrigerator. While Joanne did in fact move into that apartment, it was not without many low points and moments of trepidation.

The webs of constraint become increasingly tighter as women attempt to set up households. Race preempts the ability to live in areas of their choice, and their poverty and reliance on welfare make their choices all the more limited because they have neither economic nor social capital. Nor do they have the color capital that seemingly played an important role in the housing outcomes of White women. Take Jocelyn, for example, whose story is told in the first chapter. She easily found housing in another area outside of Laneville, within 30 days of being in the shelter. Or Lorraine, whom I briefly mentioned in chapter 5—the 30-something mother with two children. She too found housing in a more desirable town in River Valley, as did Susan, discussed in the previous chapter, who moved to another town into a trailer home. I was unaware of any Black woman who moved outside of the city of Laneville. I was also unaware of any Black woman who moved into the Downtown area. Few White women had to work as hard to find housing or work as hard within the parameters of a social serviced life as did Joanne. White women were not forced into demeaning situations with realtors and retailers because the homes they secured were not operated by landlords who removed the refrigerators.

Out-of-Reach: Revitalization and Gentrification

The second factor influencing women's housing options was the revitalization efforts that came after the economic downturn. Laneville experienced population decrease, business loss, increased filings for bankruptcy, and increased taxes during the mid-90s. Real estate sales slowed down in part because the Zytron Corporation and related industries had accounted for a large part of real estate market. One realtor said that 50% of his housing market in the late 1980s was attributable to Zytron employees. By 1993 Zytron's share dropped to 10% of his housing market. Furthermore, the resale price of homes in the county by January of 1993 fell to less than $130,000, where they had once been $140,000 or above.

On the heels of Laneville's economic revitalization (see chapter 5), the city's gentrification began, processes that Smith (1996) notes are often intersecting and simultaneous. Revitalization in Laneville was the same as it was in other cities across the country, like, for example, on the Lower East Side of Manhattan (Smith 1996) and in Harlem (Mullings and Wali 2001), where older and lower-income residents were pushed aside to meet the consumption needs of wealthier new residents. The River Valley County Economic Development Corporation has focused on increasing tourism in the area, using marketing strategies that have piqued commercial and residential investment interest, along with sparking a tourist economy.

Patterns of capital investment in Laneville are bound up in the explosion of information technology and in real estate. Commercial investment is evident, where old, once-abandoned buildings are occupied by new business. Residential rehabilitation can be seen, as older homes are refurbished and former schools transformed into lofts; cute shopping areas rise up like a phoenix out of the ashes. Revitalization efforts are encroaching upon many Black battered women's chances of locating housing in the Uptown area. Property owners and investors are interested in renovating homes and turning a profit. But real estate speculation lay within the purview of the privileged middle and upper class, most of whom are White. Gradually, more and more Whites move into Uptown, the area where primarily people of color live. Over time, the center of the city will likely become a consumer's paradise, nearby property prices will continue to escalate, and development plans will move poor people of color to more marginalized areas of the city, probably beyond the Uptown neighborhood.

Examples of how revitalization efforts restricted already fragile housing options are revealed in some of the residential development programs and funds that flowed toward the effort in Laneville. One project, established in 1993, was developed to assist working-class homeowners in refurbishing their residences, which would have helped those in Uptown. Instead, there was a shift in commitment, and the city decided to help with home purchasing; consequently, money was shifted away from the Uptown area, where a number of working-class people could have used the funds, to the already "healthy" Downtown neighborhood, making it possible for people with higher incomes to purchase homes there. After the Downtown market was saturated, potential investors sought out diamonds in the rough in Uptown, where housing remained affordable. Now, Uptown is like an excavation site for people with money who can afford to renovate, facilitated by projects that displace working-class homeowners, who often offered reasonable rental options to women and families.

The Community Housing Rehab Project was also an assistance project for working-class homeowners. Juliet, whose house is in need of repair, applied for this assistance made available only to owner-occupied dwellings. The owner/occupant must be income-eligible, and the total household income must fall within low-to-moderate income guidelines as determined by Housing and Urban Development. A family of two must make at least $23,400, but no more than $37,450. Other

qualifications include the requirement that the homeowner
must be current with property and school taxes and water
bills. Also, the title to the house must be clear. The maximum
amount of the loan is $30,000 for a multiple-family house and
$15,000 for a single-family dwelling. As we went over the
paperwork, Juliet said:

> I don't know how some homeowners are going to be
> able to access this money. Many of the people I know
> living in Uptown owe something because they are, or
> were, out of work at some point. They make it so
> hard for you. The thing is that if you apply, they
> come to your house to do an inspection. Once they
> come, if anything is in arrears, they put a lien on your
> house. Then you can't pay the lien, so people lose
> their homes. Just from applying. How's that for get-
> ting Black folk to move out?

As some residents lose their homes because of all of the obstacles presented by this program, they become available for
others to purchase. This is exactly what happened to Juliet,
who lost her family's home after the inspection due to back
taxes owed of just $800. Although homeownership programs
may be irrelevant for poor women, the relationship between
increased real estate investments and the "marking" of a space
as desirable can drive up rental prices. The impact on poor and
working-class women is that the decrease in subsidized housing increasingly excluded people from the rental market. Even
when rental developments are designated as affordable housing for low-income people, poor people's housing needs are
not factored in, and the developments are often not really
affordable when utilities and other costs are taken into
account.

Responses to Laneville's need for affordable housing have
the appearance of being suitable. An old building on the upper
northern end of Dodge Street was targeted for development by
the River Valley Housing Revival Corporation. This project is
being marketed as meeting the needs of all the community

members and was going to include retail space. Juliet was angered by this project after she discovered that the street-level retail space was slated to be a convenience store. The revitalization effort, in her opinion, should include retail stores that would meet community needs. She reasoned that a convenience store is not an example of meeting community needs because several already exist. She said, "What we need is a supermarket, where the prices are not so high. We're already poor, and when you have to shop at a convenience store, you spend more money, so they can cover their costs." As we walked to work in the rain one morning, Juliet stopped in front of the Dodge Street complex and pointed her finger. Speaking loudly she said, "How is this going to benefit us, the poorest of us?!" As it turned out, the question was very relevant, but not only because of the convenience store issue. Sara, the advocate who clued me in on the refrigerator scam, provided some insight into how poor battered women were unable to live in the new building:

> I had every battered woman fill out an application for housing at Dodge Street, while it was in the building phase. Every woman who completed the application was rejected because her income was too low. I did a calculation to see if these women could be self-sufficient. I figured out that if a woman worked a full 40-hour-a-week job, (a measurable outcome of welfare reform) at $5.35 an hour, she would make $11,128 per year. That is not enough income to qualify for an apartment at Dodge Street. That building won't do anything for poor women, and there is less and less housing available in Laneville.

New developments, which could be used for low and very low-income people, will most likely be geared toward higher-income earning households or niche populations, like artists. The city is using a Housing and Urban Development grant of $500,000 to convert a former warehouse into "affordable" (what constitutes affordable has yet to be determined) housing units with artisan lofts, gallery, and commercial space. If the deal goes through, and the application process is anything like the Dodge Street development described above, housing options for women receiving assistance still will not expand. While housing developments like Dodge Street are ostensibly for everyone, they will really be most beneficial for middle- and upper-income people.

ᘓ

Living in Laneville comes with contradictions. It is being land-scaped to attract tourists and the "overclass;" new businesses are blooming; housing in need of renovation offers exciting "homesteading" possibilities, and older buildings like schools and department stores are likely to be transformed into artists' lofts. The waterfront property is being developed, and tours abound. Loss of industry and the domino effect it had on the community was one impetus to commodify the Laneville area for the upwardly mobile (Ruben 2001). In contrast, not all have benefited from the area's prosperity. Poor women cannot afford the average fair market value of a one-bedroom apart-ment in River Valley County, which is $710 per month. To afford that type of housing, one has to have an income of $28,400 per year (National Low Income Housing Coalition 1999). The 1999 New York State TANF grant provides a single-parent family of three $579 per month. For a person with no earnings, just a TANF or Safety Net grant, the maxi-mum affordable housing cost would only be $173 per month. As gentrifying efforts take hold in Laneville, the cost of hous-ing has increased. Reading the *Laneville Journal* during Octo-ber 1998, I found 31 apartments in the city of Laneville available for rent. The average rent was $525. In just 15 months during January 2000, there were 33 listings for apart-ments in the city of Laneville, and the average rent had risen to $614, reflecting a 17% increase.

With a tight housing market and just over 40 percent of residential units owner-occupied, there was a limited pool of available rentals.[2] In addition, the quality of housing available for women on welfare is very low. The other type of housing within the permissible budget limit of RVCDSS in Laneville is public housing. The Laneville Public Housing Authority is the landlord and owner of public housing, where tenants pay 30% of their gross annual income for rent. None of the women wanted to live in public housing or in residences in run-down neighborhoods. I went to one apartment in a low-rise public housing unit. The rooms were small with cinderblock walls and looked like prison cells. The quality of the apartments was inferior, and there was a considerable amount of drug activity that women wanted to avoid. Also, women may have been hesitant to live in public housing, knowing that they may be evicted for any transgression as a result of the Housing Opportunity Program Extension Act of 1996. This Act, also signed by President Clinton has a "One Strike and You're Out Policy" that gives public housing authorities liberal rights to evict lessees who fail to monitor and restrain those living in their apartment. This includes women who are unable to restrain batterers.[3]

As a result women look for apartments they can rent using Section 8 certificates. Section 8 is a federal program that provides subsidies for low-income people to rent market-rate apartments. Renters pay a percentage of their income, and Housing and Urban Development (HUD) covers the rest. People who have tenant-based Section 8 subsidies are permitted to find their own housing units in the private housing market. Essentially, one asks a landlord if he/she is willing to be approved as a Section 8 landlord. If the landlord agrees, then an application process begins to grant Section 8 status. If one finds an apartment that accepts Section 8 subsidies, tenants pay 30% of their gross annual salary for rent. Typically, units in Laneville that accept tenant-based Section 8 subsidies are well kept and are frequently located in mixed income areas. Also, the certificate or voucher for Section 8 is portable, meaning that if you leave your current tenant-based Section 8 subsidized apartment and find a place that will accept your Section 8 subsidy, you can "port" or take your subsidy to that other location, even to a unit in another state.[4] This is an important benefit for women who are battered and have to leave the state in which they live.

However, it is nearly impossible to find a Section 8 apartment because there are 2- to 3-year-long waiting lists for certificates. Two housing administrators whom I interviewed confirmed that a three-year waiting period was the norm for a subsidized apartment. The county has about 800 Section 8 units, the city of Laneville has approximately 500 units, and Laneville Housing Authority has 35 units. Most of these subsidized units are occupied. Existing levels of subsidized housing do not meet the need because low-income rentals are scarce, and the price of housing has inched up after being deflated in the early 1990s. In March 2000 the city of Laneville Section 8 Program approved searches for subsidized apartments for people who had applied in 1997.

One relationship between Section 8 housing and welfare reform is located in the sanctioning process, which according to Irene, the Section 8 Housing Administrator, has meant an increase in the number of women coming to the Section 8 office. She explains:

> I would say the number of women we see has increased. A lot of women . . . what happens now is that you're a woman on public assistance. They sanction you. You're off the grant. So now you're living off less money . . . so realistically, you can't pay your rent, and you owe. You can't afford it. Now you're going to be evicted. So now you're going to come to me because you need me. I can't take you because we don't take people that owe back rent. You have to be current, plus we don't do emergency housing. So, it all falls back on DSS again, because they are going to end up putting you in a shelter and the cost of a shelter, do you know what it costs? $68 per day for each person. Something like that. It's outrageous. Does that make sense to you? $1,800 a month to be in a homeless shelter, and they're not going to pay your back rent for you, which could be 600 bucks?

Affordable housing is so desperately needed in Laneville that Jayson, a young Black man in his 20s, capitalized on the dearth by acting as an unofficial screening agent. I met Jayson when I got into his cab one morning. He looked very familiar, but I could not place him. A discussion ensued about how he came to Laneville, and what he did for a living besides driving a cab. We met several times over the course of 2 months, and he told me how, due to lack of earnings, he set up a business with a landlord who owned a building in his neighborhood. The landlord did not like placing ads in the paper and did not want to use a realtor to rent vacant apartments. But, he also wanted someone help him rent vacancies to particular kinds of women, (no men); none with rowdy children or with boyfriends that would cause trouble. This is where Jayson came in. Acting as a screener on the landlord's behalf, Jayson hung around the Department of Social Services (this is why he looked familiar when we first met in the cab), watching women to determine their "eligibility" for an apartment in "his" building. Searching for "flaws," like drug use, potentially problematic male partners, or women with lots of children, Jayson screened them out. He was sort of keen on moms with one kid, so if she passed his "test," then he would strike up a conversation to find out the candidate's housing needs. If he liked the woman and thought she would make a good tenant, arrangements were made to see the apartment. In return women paid him a "finders fee" and then the landlord paid him as well.

Recovery of neglected neighborhoods, like Uptown, means that poor people are being rendered invisible. It seems on the surface that renovation and revitalization is a good thing. It's just that women like Leslie and Joanne may not get to experience that transformation, as their rents increase, but their incomes don't. When their benefits run out due to the time limits imposed by welfare reform law, and if they still have not found permanent employment, where will they go? Even if they find employment, will the wages be enough to support living in a revitalized Laneville? Ruben (2001) claims that development strategies are worsening poor people's opportunities, as investments in the city bypass them in favor of promoting growth and prosperity. Ultimately, what happens is that poor residents lapse into the background, while cities become homogenized.

The confluence of forced evictions (due to violence), unaffordable housing (due to privatization and elite reclamation of property), and unavailable housing (due to violence and or residential racialization) in Laneville are forms of violence that take on new shape in the lives of battered Black women. Unlike Black women, White women were able to move into apartments in other parts of the county and in nicer neighborhoods in Laneville with far greater ease than their Black counterparts were. One reason was that many of the White women had cars. The other reason was that as White women, they enjoyed the privilege of color capital in the real estate market, expanding their housing options. Women like Leslie and Joanne had difficulty finding housing in general and especially housing that they wanted; some places simply would not rent apartments to Black women, as evidenced by what happened when Leslie and I went house-hunting. Yet, women like Jocelyn, and even Susan, a 36-year-old White woman with six children, were more likely to be able to move out of the city center of Laneville into Downtown and other areas of River Valley.

8

Strategic Missions

Limited access to resources stimulates the development of survival strategies to make up for scarcity. When the solution to poverty is market based, and the market deepens one's poverty, survival becomes germane. In the absence of realizing security through the state, women attempt to stabilize fluctuations in the resources they had available at any given moment. The emphasis on sanctioning recipients and the single-minded focus of work was often counter-productive, as women experienced shortfalls and crises, and expended a great deal of their time and resources responding to them.

We must turn our attention to the ways in which Black women act against constraints. How do Black women who are battered and poor survive the poverty and displacement brought about by abuse and policy sanctions? I found that during and after the shelter experience, even when they are situated in their own homes, women continued to experience hardships in terms of finances, housing, and child care because government assistance was so tenuous. Since poor women have rarely been able to survive on welfare payments, they have always had to construct survival strategies. I was able to observe four strategies deployed by the women whose lives I have examined in this study. Each served to help women create stable households and families despite the constraints they faced. These strategies included: the creation of fictive kin support networks; the development of instrumental relationships; the use of speech acts; and engagement in illegalities. While they are discussed independently, this in no way suggests that women employ only one strategy at a time, as they use as many as are necessary at any given moment. Evidence of these strategies have come up at various points in this ethnography. For example, in chapter 5, when I discuss the risks women like Gina and Joelle took, I note that they were willing to or did engage in criminal survival activities. Gina was forced to consider prostitution, while Joelle sold drugs because they were unable to earn enough money in the wage labor market.

In this chapter, I present the strategies alluded to in previous chapters as coherent responses to the overlapping spheres in which welfare reform policy has an affect on women's needs during and after their shelter stay. In discussing these survival strategies, I note that they are all responses to abuse *and* poverty. Some are intended to address poverty; others are particular to the experiences of abuse. However, these strategies are now being deployed at this particular historical moment characterized by a sharp decline in public sector resources dedicated to serving the poor. So they are discussed as broad responses formed at the intersection of poverty, race, and violence. In the lives of these women, these overlapping experiences cannot be readily separated into categories. I would argue that each of the strategies used reflects how this group of women invent responses to deal with the external events that make life so hard, and dangerous.

Creating Fictive Kin

Since most of the women spent up to 3 months at the shelter, they came to know each other very well, and the relationships they developed lasted well beyond shelter life. Because the escalation of violence in women's lives caused family ties to disintegrate, women like Clemmie (whose life story is told at the beginning of this ethnography) attempted to recreate the family that was lost due to violence. What she wanted to do was to build a safe home for her children and to restore the sense of family she had lost. The challenge of accomplishing this goal was exacerbated by the fact that Clemmie needed a new identity for herself, since her batterer could locate her through her social security number. Without a new social security number, Clemmie was unable to secure a job and could not get utilities turned on in her name. She was dependent upon RVCDSS and the Social Security Administration to make a decision as to whether or not a new identity was possible. Although the process for changing Clemmie's social security number was initiated the same month she arrived at the shelter in November of 1998, Clemmie had heard nothing by February of 1999, when it was time for her to leave the shelter to move into her own place, which she ultimately did.

Clemmie wanted to reconstitute the family she so missed and did what many women do while at the shelter—she constructed a network of individuals who became her new family of choice. She is not the only woman at the shelter to have done this, but hers was the most substantively developed network. Her network was composed of staff and shelter residents. As she described it to me:

> Margaret, (a shelter advocate) is like a grandmother to my children. Josie (a resident) is like my daughter—cause she's so close in age to Shawnice. Her daughter Shaneva is my granddaughter, and I'm gonna teach her everything she needs to know about being Black—since her father is Black and she don't see him. Sheila is my sister. She's the person who makes me feel like a family. I know when she's sad, and she trusts me. I miss my baby sister, so she's her for now. Alfonso, [a male advocate] is James and Henry's dad, and Sheila's son Marcel is like a younger brother to Henry because he needs someone to look up to him; especially since he is so far away from his younger cousins.

Members of Clemmie's fictive kin family were not only Black women from the shelter but also included White shelter staff and Josie the young White woman referred to earlier. An argument could be made that need blurred the lines of race, because when it came to "making family" to help through lean times, race and ethnic divisions were the least of her concerns.

By April of 1999, Clemmie was still unable to work due to the unresolved Social Security number issue and had spent a considerable amount of time at the RVCDSS office getting one waiver after another, always reminding the staff that working under her old Social Security number was too dangerous. At this point Clemmie was receiving $450 toward her $500 rent; $104 in cash and $171 in food stamps each month. She clearly needed more money because the $171 did not cover food costs for the five people living in her household. Of the $104 in cash she received, Clemmie used $50 to cover the difference between her rent and her subsidy, and $54 for food, bringing her total food expenditure up to $225 a month. This amounted to $45 per person or $1.50 per day for everybody. After those two expenses (rent and food), Clemmie had no money left. She had no money to bring her daughter home from college, no money to get clothes for the kids, or to pay the phone bill. Clemmie had to find a way to access funds. The following field notes illustrate how Clemmie survived using the fictive kin network she created while at the shelter:

April 1999

Clemmie's small apartment was full of people; her daughter was lying across one of two old couches in the cramped living room watching the "Maury Povich" show. Her niece was sitting on the other couch doing her hair. Henry, Clemmie's son, was playing and tugging at Clemmie's shirt, informing her that he was about to go downstairs and ride his bike. In the middle of the room stood Josie (who used to be at the shelter) holding Shaneva. "Remember her, that's my daughter and that's my granddaughter," Clemmie said. Of course I remembered Josie. As she walked toward the door, Josie slipped Clemmie some money. Looks like $20. Josie hugged Clemmie goodbye and left.

Clemmie asked if I wanted something to drink as we sat in the kitchen, the only room large enough for more than three people to be in comfortably and have some elbow room. We sat in the kitchen for hours. She talked about her newly found connection to Jehovah and her recent visit with her caseworker at Social Services, who threatened to cut her benefits. After a while, I finally asked her about the money Josie gave her, and Clemmie told me the details of how she made money baby-sitting for women in her network:

> All I want now is help with my rent. I'm not trying to get them [RVCDSS] to help me live. I always had it in my mind to get my own money. I'm not trying to buy furniture, chandeliers, and keep sneakers on my kid's feet 'cause I can work to do that. I'm just up on my own two feet, so I need a little help. 'So, how do you do it?' I asked. Sheila [her "sister"] gives me $60 a week for watching Marcel from 4 to 6:15 pm 5 days a week. But she's struggling, I know I could get more than that but I got to help my "sister" out. She can't give me any more. She gives me what she can give me. For Josie, [her "daughter"] I may watch the baby one day on the weekend, she'll bring me $20. I tell her no, but she insists. I also watch Linda's [another former resident] son. She has to work at the burger place 'cause DSS wouldn't give her anything. She works the midnight to eight shift, so he just sleeps over here. She pays me $50. I never thought about making a living doing the childcare thing. I used to make $11 something an hour working construction. But now, how I'm gonna live off of $52 every two weeks? What's that gonna do? Anything that keeps money coming in, that's regular, I'll do it.

Clemmie earned $130 a week from her baby-sitting jobs. The fictive kin network established months before contributed to her subsistence, without which she would have been unable to take care of her children. The ethnographic literature shows that cross-culturally, women draw on kin networks to cope

with privation. Family networks and patterns of exchange have
been widely discussed as a mechanism for accessing material
resources, services, and information, which can influence family
members' standards of living (Mencher 1993; Dehavenon and
Okongwu 1993). The creation of fictive kin is a particularly
useful way to understand how obligation and resource-sharing
transcend blood ties. Drawing from Stack's seminal book, *All
Our Kin* (1974), it is clear that the ability to survive poverty is
facilitated by the formation of informal links that have little to
do with being related by blood.

Children at the shelter also created fictive kin relations with
women, sometimes independent of their mothers' involvement.
This occurred between the children of Angela, a non-English-
speaking shelter resident, and Sherita, the African-American
woman in her 30s who moved to River Valley County after
leaving her husband and was later beaten by her boyfriend,
Joey. Angela's children, Elmo and Eugenia, translated the Eng-
lish-speaking world for their mother. They also used her inability to speak English to manipulate her into thinking that
shelter staff had given them permission to do things they actually had not received permission for, such as going out. Fortu-
nately, staff quickly recognized the children were playing them
off against their mother and subsequently deferred to her at all
times with regard to where the children could and could not
go, and with whom. Through trial and error, the children discovered which residents their mother approved of, and ultimately they crafted an alliance with Sherita, who became their
"aunt." With their "aunt" as a chaperone, the children
increased their freedom of movement around Laneville.

The relationship between Sherita and Angela's children
continued after both women had moved out of the shelter,
which suited all of them just fine. Angela wanted the children
to have an adult they could look up to and trust, given the
trauma of having had their home life disrupted. And "Aunt"
Sherita was more than pleased to have an instant family for

whom she had some responsibility and with whom she could have some fun. Elmo, Eugenia, and Sherita went shopping. Elmo and Eugenia were permitted to spend the night at Sherita's, especially if they were going to a party. Sometimes they just hung out. Once a week they all had dinner at Sherita's.

Sherita's "aunt" status came with one condition; she had to operate within the parameters of the rules laid out by Angela. It was Sherita who was responsible for making sure the children called home to let their mother know where they were or Sherita had to call on their behalf. In return, when Sherita was low on food stamps or when they were reduced, Angela sent meals over to her.

Fictive kinship worked to smooth the uncertainties of nonpayment, sanctions, and benefit reductions (as was the case with Sherita). The relationships helped women who were unemployed (Clemmie) and those who were employed but lacked child care, like Sheila, whose need to work ended up exploiting women like Clemmie as cheap sources of child care, a common pattern also documented by Salzinger (1997). Financial uncertainties were resolved in large measure through monetary and in-kind exchanges among network members. Women's survival depended on these networks, and they were aware of the responsibility that came with being integrated into one. One caution, of course, is that although networks are connected to a sense of obligation, they can and do expand and contract. The threads of kin- or fictive kin-based networks can be stretched quite thin, especially when women have limited resources to share with all the people in their fictive kin circle.

Instrumental Friendships

Some women found themselves in the position of having to develop instrumental friendships, intentionally entering into functional relationships with both noninstitutionally and institutionally affiliated individuals. They were people from whom the women could get something if they needed to, and the relationship was constructed most often by women who had not developed fictive kin relations with other women while at the shelter.

Landlords, grocery store owners, and bus drivers, are examples of noninstitutionally affiliated individuals with whom women formed alliances. The relationship was usually initiated by a woman who often performed a "favor" for a person. The favor was "banked" as form of credit in the event they needed something in the future. Beth, a White woman in her 40s who works with battered women, shared her observations with me about how instrumental relationships operate using the example of landlords:

> They find ways to be a good tenant. They will make sure that everything is clean, or quiet, or something to please their landlords, so he/she will like them and give them slack. One woman had a small clerical job [along with receiving TANF funds]. She made friends with the landlord up front, and he liked her. She was conscientious about keeping her apartment and the rest of the building clean. She was very careful. And then whenever she had to have her car repaired, she knew she wouldn't also be able to pay her rent on time, she was able to negotiate with the landlord. I know that the landlord applied for and got that apartment registered to accept Section 8 subsidies. The rules for Section 8 include timely payment of rent. With that, she should have been paying her rent on time, but the landlord let her keep the arrangement of paying when she could. I just don't know how long these things will last.

After moving into their apartments, many women informally and unofficially took on the role of maintenance person or groundskeeper. If the hallway light bulb blew out, they would purchase a replacement drawing from their own limited funds. Or, without being asked, they would organize the garbage for pick-up, making sure that the recycled garbage was in the correct bag or placing other tenants' garbage in the appropriate place. Occasionally, women planted flowers or tended to the landlord's garden. They did these things with no expectation of monetary payment, and the landlords never, to my knowledge, offered to repay them. Sherita, Clemmie, Joanne, and other women living in owner-occupied or units in houses extended their "services" to their landlords. Each took on some building maintenance work knowing that there was no accounting for what they "spent," but in the end, even though they did not expect money, they expected something in return. They were building up moral credit, looking good in the eyes of people they did not know intimately, but from whom they could request a favor at some point. The women expected that their good deeds done would be leveraged against a future need. Sherita, for example, prepared meals for the owner of a small grocery store and expected that she could buy food using the moral credit she had previously banked, when her food stamps were reduced or eliminated.

The women in this ethnography lived by the art of making arrangements (Pardo 1996), and these instrumental friendships were defined in terms of how deficits could be managed (Wolf 1966). This was a necessary strategy in light of how often women were sanctioned, how they experienced benefit reductions, or how they just could not make ends meet no matter how hard they tried. In its practicality, instrumental friendships draw on the burden of emotion in which an uneven set of performances of assistance are exchanged.

These engagements are tenuous for several reasons. First, if a woman does not provide a favor, the potential alliance is terminated. Second, the relationship does not exist between equals, as the woman is in a subordinate position and risks being exploited. As Wolf states, "the relation contains an element which provides sanctions internal to the relation itself" (Wolf 1966: 13). In other words the relationship between a giver and a receiver is limited, because the giver has power upon which the receiver depends. Further, this type of relationship does not change a woman's status from being poor, although it does alleviate a particular resource dearth at a particular moment. Clearly the alliances women developed came with the hope that the person or donor would have enough sympathy to assist them when it became necessary.

Expressions of assistance on the part of the "donor" were considered more substantial than simply a favor. Aid offered by the "donor" was crucial to women's survival because without it, women might go hungry or lose their apartments. Relationships of this type developed out of need mostly because women's support networks were thin or nonexistent.

Speech Acts

Words are a forceful mediator for people living on the margins of society (Desjarlais 1997), and women told stories in an attempt to offer a subjective perspective on their situation. Sharing details of their lives are intended to manage the stigma of being on welfare and being perceived as fraudulent, exemplified partially by Gloria's talk as described in chapter 4. Women also used speech acts to persuade people to help them, where talking has a use-value in a calculated exchange process. Sociolinguists distinguish between what is known as ordinary and institutional conversation (see Labov 1972; Drew and Heritage 1992), although there are critiques about categorizing conversation in this way (McElhinny 1997) because it limits the ways in which people's talk can cross over at any given point. However, the categorization is a useful point of departure in understanding the composition of different kinds of conversation. Ordinary conversation is that which involves nonstandard speech patterns and familiar talk. Institutional conversation is characterized by a core goal or task, and there are constraints on what participants can say (McElhinny 1997:

110). However, the speech acts in which many Black women engaged show that desperation oftentimes produces the use of more familiar, ordinary talk in institutional spaces. We see the interplay of these two types of talk in relation to the speech acts deployed by Sherita when her benefits were reduced.

✍

Sherita never intended to be on social services for long. In fact, all she really wanted was medical coverage. Over a 2-month period, Sherita's plan for economic autonomy nearly came to a halt, when some of her benefits were cut off and others reduced:

> They [social services] don't see that a person who gets on temporary, means temporary. Temporary means short-term assistance . . . until I got myself back on my feet and got a full-time job. They sent me 100 letters a week. In fact the more I progressed, the more they stayed on my back. I really needed the Medicaid. But they cut that off.

Sherita's benefit reduction occurred in two stages. The first was just before she completed a training program to become a Certified Nursing Assistant. The second occurred 2 months after she finished the program. Her motivation was commendable, for while she was in the training program, she had surgery on her eye, and then returned to work at a discount store one week later. More hours were available because it was the holiday season, and in agreeing to work additional hours, her paychecks were increased—$250 one week and $200 another. Sherita's usual take-home pay was about $150 per week. As a result of these extra earnings, her grant was reduced to $23 from $350 because she had worked overtime during the holiday season and made "too much money" to qualify for full Safety Net funding.

RVCDSS reduced Sherita's benefits in the middle of December in 1998, shortly after she moved into her apartment and just before she finished the training program in which she was enrolled. She was very worried about paying her rent for the month of January and had no idea how she was going to pay her utilities.

> I was doing everything. They wanted me to work full time but I was in training 3-1/2 hours a day. Then I would go to work. Then they put me in a CWEP [Community Work Employment Program], which meant I had to work off my grant. I go to school, I go to CWEP, and to work. Every other weekend I would work 12 hours. The money would add up, and they figured I was making too much, so they cut me off. They cut me off, and I wasn't sturdy, you know. That's not helping somebody.

Sherita made several arrangements using speech acts. The first thing she did was walk down to the real estate office that managed her building and told the office assistant, in great detail, everything that had happened to her. She told the assistant about leaving her husband, moving to River Valley County, that she was let go from her job at Zytron Corporation, how she moved in with Joey, his drug use, and his physical abuse. This is one of Sherita's greatest survival techniques. She would tell almost anyone anything about her life in order to have her basic needs met. After telling her story, Sherita asked the assistant if she could make her rent payment in two installments, once on the 10th and again on the 30th of each month. The assistant, who had "always been nice," told her she could pay the rent "half and half . . . and that's what I've been doing." But the arrangement was informal, and there was no promise that the management agency would never ask Sherita for the rent to be paid all at once on the first of the month. Furthermore, Sherita was unaware at the time that she would be charged late fees. Sherita was billed $20 late fees for several months and had not realized it because she physically delivered her rent payment to the real estate office to cut down on the cost of postage and never paid attention to the bill that came in the mail.

Sherita also phoned her "vendors" as she called them. The cable, phone, and electricity companies were contacted. She informed each vendor of everything that happened to her—the beatings, the loss of her job, her participation in the CNA training program, and the reduction of her benefits: "Meanwhile, the electricity, cable, and the phone bill had to be paid. I had a place to stay, but the lights . . . they (Social Services) don't care if I can't see. Cable is considered a luxury to them. But that's my only entertainment 'cause I'm too scared to go out." I asked the Commissioner of River Valley County Department of Social Services about the problems recipients have when their grants are cut in the middle of their process toward "self-sufficiency" and pointed out that as soon as they make $1.00 more than the allowable amount, their benefits are cut off. Consequently, they fall behind and cannot catch up. He acknowledged this was a problem of the system:

> That's certainly a place where our system is lacking. If you are going to make enough money in one month to make you ineligible, your case is going to be closed. Now there is the 46% disregard, so one can make more money that first month than you would normally get. But if you are going to go 200% above the poverty line, you're not eligible for any money. There is nothing in our system that says, 'keep your first month's pay and use that first month to get ahead . . .' If your landlord is used to getting the full rent on the first, and now you're only getting half of your grant, you can't possibly pay your rent. So now, unless you have a very lenient landlord, you're at best going to have late charges. No, our system isn't set up to let a person get a boost to get going.

Shortly after graduating from the training program at the end of December 1998, Sherita obtained a position at a nursing home and left the discount store where she had been employed. That job was part-time and did not come with benefits. Sherita was able to keep Medicaid, but then 2 months later, in February 1999, it was cut off, and she never found out why. No letter was sent informing her that her Medicaid would be suspended. Sherita wanted and, in fact, needed to keep Medicaid because she was not working full-time, and she still needed to have dental work completed from when she had been beaten and had her teeth dislodged. Again, she employed speech acts to get her medical needs met.

Sherita went to see Mrs. Thompson, the woman at the nursing home who had hired her. She described how she had been beaten, which resulted in some of her teeth being dislodged. Sherita made it a point to emphasize how important it was to have a professional smile.

> With any new job, I wouldn't have health benefits. My health issues are my teeth and my eyes, especially my eyes. Since I had the surgery, my eye is still not all that great. It doesn't focus great. I still get headaches. That was why I wanted to keep the Medicaid. I didn't get everything I needed done.

With her Medicaid suspended and faced with her need for health coverage, Sherita talked her supervisor into speeding up the benefit process by one month to ensure she would have coverage. Sherita's strategy of telling people everything about herself was, in some ways, manipulative, using the power of the confessional to achieve positive outcomes in the form of badly needed goods and services. As their experiences became known through the use of speech acts, many women felt they could influence the course of their own lives.

Debbie, a housing administrator, described the impact women's speech acts had on her. She told me that when poor women came to her office, sat down, cried, and told her every detail of their lives, which they frequently did, she was moved. "Many of them tell their whole life story as a negotiating point to get a place to live." Debbie admitted that she views the women a little differently afterward, more as individuals and less the stereotype of a "Welfare Queen," and to the degree possible, she tried to find housing for those women first.

Although many times the other party was noninstitutional personnel, such as a housing/rental agent, women also used speech acts with social service caseworkers. Clemmie, for example, deployed a speech act by begging in an attempt to convince the job counselor at RVCDSS to rescind the decision that Shawnice, Clemmie's 19-year-old daughter could not attend River Valley County Community College, but should be working. As discussed in chapter 5, welfare reform policy does not permit recipients to attend community college, except for 20% of a municipality's caseload, so Shawnice was mandated to work or participate in work-related activity, unlike, I might add, Josie. The educational program in which Shawnice was enrolled did not qualify as one of the allowable work-related or educational programs.

When the job counselor informed Clemmie and Shawnice that the focus of welfare was on work and not education, Clemmie explained to the woman how she had raised all of her children to achieve academically. She discussed how much effort she put into exposing the children to different experiences and providing them educational activities. She shared with her caseworker her younger daughter's college success story; that she had received a full scholarship to a private school, and that both of her sons were in gifted programs at their new schools. Then, in what Clemmie describes as her most embarrassing moment, she got down on her knees and begged the social service caseworker to not penalize the family financially because Shawnice was in school and not working full time. Clemmie did not experience a benefit reduction on that day, but did lose her benefits one month later in May of 1999.

Talking takes on an urgency that emerges from dire circumstances in which women use the "confessional" as one way of coping with poverty and coping with structural impediments that predictably deepened women's actual and perceived fears of poverty. Their disclosures, however, are not a reflection of democratic speech situations. Confessions are compelled by the need to survive and express the nature of power differentials between the speech "actor" and the listener. When women use speech acts with realtors, caseworkers, and employers, they participate in unequal relations of power, where the listener judges their worthiness. This relationship is entered into in part because welfare reform exacerbates the subordinate position from which poor women must operate from in order to get what they need. They confess because they have to, not because they want to, and sometimes self-exposure is humiliating, as is evident in Clemmie's situation.

In their own interpretation of narrating their lives due to circumstances beyond their control, some women directly stated that their "soliloquies" were definitely intended to shift the scales of uncertainty in their favor. As Sherita put it, talking was: ". . . a necessary manipulation. How else are they gonna know anything about me? . . . I have a real story, and they need to know who I am, not what they think I am."

Interviews with community advocates revealed there has been an increase in the use of speech acts as a survival strategy since welfare reform. Helen, an advocate who has been doing community work for 15 years, told me that welfare reform has caused women to really think through the kinds of arrangements they may need because of a crisis:

> They talk their landlords into letting them pay the rent in small portions. They say 'Next Monday, I'll give so and so amount.' They can't do this at the big complexes, they can only do it with private homeowners. Of course this limits women's choices for housing because they have to live in smaller buildings, like private homes, where they can negotiate with landlords.

❦

Occasionally speech acts were so startling that initially women received a positive response because the listener was so shocked by what he/she heard. However, later the initial determination was rescinded. In Solange's case, her desperation lay in not wanting to return to her husband. Solange refused to live through her husband's "sickness" again—lining toothpicks up against the front door to determine if she had left the house when he was not home. She was determined to find housing, but was having difficulty. Maybe it was because she was a Black woman on her own with two children.

Solange, age 37, is a former foster child who had survived child sexual abuse for many years. The horrors of child sexual abuse festered into bulimia, according to Solange. As no one believed her early on she found that institutional personnel responded not to her sexual violence, but to her bulimia. "My bulimia gives me a sense of control. I don't stick my finger down my throat like the others do. I just cough until my food comes up. But I've got it under control now. But I know when it's coming, it happens when I get anxious." While living in Laneville, Solange's quest for housing was challenging—maybe due to the hidden hand of racism, but Solange had a comeback to those who told her, "We have nothing available." She confessed that she had bulimia. She would hold her chest and begin coughing, then with shortened breath, she would say, "my bulimia is coming on." Solange preferred to find a Section 8 rental apartment and was unwilling to accept the DSS housing assistance because she did not want to live in a "slum." To appease Solange, the secretary at the Section 8 office told her to absolutely fill out an application for a Section 8 apartment, which of course immediately stabilized her on-coming bulimic attack. On Solange's part this was a desperate attempt to capture control where there was none, to circumvent homelessness and reestablish a household for herself and her daughters.

Having no safe place to live was one of the biggest fears the women faced and talking one's way into an apartment does make sense. But sometimes Solange's speech acts were misdirected. For example, I know she thought I had some power to influence her entry into an apartment complex that was coowned by Angel House and the River Valley Housing Authority. Twice she told me how her condition could be neutralized, if she knew she could get into the supportive housing program, coughing for the duration of the conversation. The routine of reminding those around her that her bulimia was triggered by anxiety was a different way of telling her story to bring about a positive outcome, and she believed that if narrated and performed well enough to the right person, a deal might be struck putting the odds in her favor.

Gal (1991) points out that in sharing personal details about oneself, the listener will judge your worthiness, which was precisely the women's intent. Women's verbal practices are an effort to represent their own experiences, and speech acts offer women the opportunity to provide a version of who they are, what their needs are. Simultaneously, by speaking up, they are contesting institutional inadequacies, which have failed them.

Successful response rates from talking motivated most women to continue using speech acts to help them get their needs met. Whom they chose to disclose to is as important as what they chose to disclose. Typically it was to formal institutional network personnel, such as social service caseworkers, public housing authority staff, advocates, and employers. It was someone whom they thought could offer immediate help and was rarely used in situations when the women felt less certain of the outcome. Most of the Black women used the confessional to convince and persuade those in power that they were indeed worthy of assistance. But one woman, whose story is told below, refused to talk.

Illegalities

"I hate the publicness of my life," said Elizabeth. "It is demeaning to have to prove yourself over and over again, and I won't do it!" This is one of the first comments that Elizabeth, a Black woman in her 30s, made to me when I asked her about

welfare, welfare reform, and her interactions with social services. "I don't want this ever again."

The kind of publicizing of their lives that most of the
women so fully engaged in outraged Elizabeth. Some of it had
to do with the way she was raised—in a family that never
revealed very much to each other. Elizabeth was born in the
West Indies and raised in Great Britain. Her family, which con-
sisted of her mother, father, and five siblings, came to live in
New York when she was 6 years old. Elizabeth was gifted and
received a full scholarship to attend a prestigious, all-girls, private high school, followed by attendance at a prestigious university on the East Coast.

Elizabeth's refusal to share her personal life and her needs
almost made her a mystery at the shelter. She would leave the
shelter and not inform staff of her whereabouts which was met
with "eviction warnings." She seemed to like me, and I became
the person appointed to try and find out where she was going.
All she would ever tell me was that she was going out because
she had "business to take care of."

Elizabeth has two children, Kamari, 5 and Olu, age 3, by
her husband John who is a disabled veteran. Kamari has severe
eczema and a learning disability, and Olu has severe asthma.
The boys are her pride and joy, and every breath she takes, she
told me, is taken toward ensuring that their lives are stabilized.

After 2 weeks of missing each other at the shelter, we
finally sat down in the television room at the shelter one afternoon. The backdrop to our conversation was The Ricki Lake
show, where the drama of everyday life unfolded in 60 minutes. It took considerably more time for Elizabeth's own life
history to unfold. But the most important thing she told me
was that her husband had been awarded court-ordered visitation rights and had seen his sons somewhat regularly over the
past 3 years since their separation. Elizabeth tried to include
John in decisions about their children, the oldest of whom was
having difficulty in school. One evening she took Olu with her
when she went to speak with John about some issues Kamari
was having at school. John started yelling at her and blaming
her for Kamari's problems. His rage turned physical, and he

picked Elizabeth up and held her up against the wall by her neck in front of Olu. Choking, she says, she begged him to stop and finally wrangled free from his grip. She and Olu ran out of the house into a cab that happened to be cruising by.

Knowing that this would trigger a flight response on Elizabeth's part, John called her later that night threatening to "get her," if she took the children someplace where he could not see them. Of course she was concerned about what he might do to her, and Elizabeth came to Angel House.

Elizabeth arrived at Angel House with an open DSS case from New York City. She had been on social services since shortly after the birth of her youngest son due to his asthma. The frequency of his attacks caused her to lose her job as a community worker. Although it took a while to kick in, Elizabeth received unemployment until it ran out, and then applied for and received social services and Medicaid. She also had Section 8 housing and tried to "port" it to Laneville, but it was explained to me by a community worker that River Valley County really did all it could to prevent women from other parts of New York from receiving benefits from the county.

While at the shelter, Elizabeth began her search to locate a place to live that would be safe for her and her children, but with no success. She started to feel that she would not be able to create a life for herself and her kids if she stayed in New York because she was unable to find a place to live. On several occasions, Elizabeth told me that she would be willing to move out-of-state, in spite of the fact that the children's father threatened to have her arrested. She said: "I don't think I have a choice. I think making enough money to buy a plane ticket to Great Britain is what I might have to do. The children don't have dual citizenship, but I do. As soon as I hit British soil, there will be a support system, not like here." Elizabeth had tremendous disdain for the U.S. welfare system. She had been treated with hostility when she had gone to apply for assistance in New York City prior to coming to the shelter.

I had lost my job. I didn't have any money, and my unemployment had not kicked in. We had run out of food supplies, and medical bills for my son were piling up. I went to Social Services in New York City. I walked there every day hoping to get an emergency check. I had no money, so I had to beg the bus drivers to let me on the bus, so I could drop off and pick up my Kamari at school. He was going to school in one borough, and we lived in another borough. Then every day for a week, I walked there. It rained that whole week. Every day they wouldn't have a check for me. The worker would laugh in my face and tell me, 'Tomorrow, it will be ready tomorrow.' Finally, I told them that if they didn't give me an emergency check, I would camp out there, and they would have to call the police. I developed a deep hatred for public assistance. I'd rather leave the country than go to Social Services.

After 3 months of trying to reestablish a household in Laneville, Elizabeth decided to move to Michigan, an area where she felt she could be comfortable and could pursue work. In so doing, she would be in violation of the court-mandated visitation agreement handed down on behalf of her husband. In spite of the fact that the boys' father had threatened to have her arrested, she decided that she would "rather be a fugitive." Elizabeth's decision to "be a fugitive" not only resulted from wanting to get away from her husband, but also "to get away from the eyes of the system." In order to get the services she needed to rebuild her life, she would have to tell her story; Elizabeth was unconvinced that the system was effective enough to warrant such self-exposure.

Because one goal of welfare reform was to reduce the numbers of people receiving assistance, it seemed to be bureaucratic ineffectiveness that prevented Elizabeth from being able to determine her own life. Of course diversionary tactics frustrate people so much that they want to end the application process and are an effective mechanism for roll reduction.

Refusal to help propelled the women to think in survival terms, but their activities could more often than not be defined in criminal terms. Other women in Laneville survived by engaging in illegal activities. For example, pregnant teens were being forced to live illegal lives, since welfare law does not permit them to receive assistance. One 18-year old young woman in particular, who was unable to access social services because of her age, refused to go home where the threat of violence was ever present. She needed a place to stay and lived illegally in a building in Laneville, until the landlord discovered she was sleeping in the basement. The space was uninhabitable, but she lived there out of desperation with no heat or electricity. Her marginal existence was precipitated by policy that wanted to force her to return to her parents' house, which was not a safe environment.

Other women who lived this way were Latina immigrants, who had tremendous difficulty renting apartments because they were Latina. Several advocates shared how difficult it was for Latina women, especially, to secure a job or an apartment. Giselle, a Spanish-speaking battered women's advocate, told me:

> The women will live wherever they can. One woman paid money to sleep on a mattress behind a couch in the living room where eight other people lived. That was her apartment. They do these things that aren't legal like rent out space from others because they can't afford to survive with the low payment from Social Services. Or, because they can't get on social services because it is too hard to apply.

Most people operate from a series of truths about their lives on which their actions are based, and for all the women in this ethnography, the Black women in particular, desperation for safety and economic solvency was one truth that forced them to make the choices they did. Within a range of options that moved along a continuum from transgressive to illegal, some of the women engaged in strategies in an attempt to secure access to material resources. For example, some women sustained contact with former batterers—a transgression that could be met with repercussion if they had taken out an order of protection. Contact was sustained primarily for the purpose of ensuring child care, precipitated by the threat of sanction and by work mandates.

However women risked losing their children or being charged with endangering the life of a minor, if the father was known to the court or Department of Social Services to be a batterer. But several women made these arrangements, so they could attend mandatory training programs or work. In exchange, the women promised to not ask for child support because in their view, child support was the child care the fathers of their children provided. Several advocates suggested that women also may be less likely to request orders of protection from their abusers because they were so desperate for child care.

A variation of illegalities is revealed in what happened at Clemmie's house 4 months after she moved into her apartment. Shortly before Clemmie lost her benefits, and I am sure she anticipated the cut-off, she and her daughters all ended up with boyfriends. I was perplexed at the new household structure. My fieldnotes from that day read as follows:

June 1999
I rang the bell, and Clemmie looked out the window and said, "Who?" "It's Dana," I said. She came down to open the door and invited me up. "Everybody's still asleep," she told me. We walked in the front door and on the couches were each of her daughters, wrapped around their respective boyfriends. Clemmie and I went into her room. "Who are those people?" I asked. "That's their boyfriends. I don't really like that they are

here, but what can I say?" I said, "You could tell them they can't come here." Rumor around the shelter had it that all of the men in Clemmie's house were dealing drugs, including Clemmie's new boyfriend. I asked her how he was treating her. "Oh, he's the best thing that ever happened to me. He treats me real nice and buys us stuff." I asked if he was dealing [drugs], to which she responded, "I don't think so. He was, but we talked about it, and he's been looking for a real job. But I know those boys are dealing. I don't want that up in my house."

I suggested that we walk to the store. "I don't have any money," she said. "Could you get me a pack of cigarettes?" Of course I obliged. It was a beautiful morning. Laneville was not buzzing with activity yet, so we sat down on a bench in a park that Clemmie chose. "I come here when I need to get away from them all," she told me. "I just love this place. It's my secret place." She looked away from me, and there were tears in her eyes. Clemmie said she felt so helpless about the girls. "They ain't never been with guys like that before. I don't know why they doing this now. I want to stop them, but I don't know how. It hurts me that they are in this."

I had heard from Sherita that Clemmie had been cut off from TANF. They had run into each other at Social Services about a month before. Sherita said Clemmie was wondering how she was going to survive. It seems that the new boyfriends were helping out with that. They bought food sometimes, and the girls got to go out. Clemmie's boyfriend also contributed to the household.

I asked Clemmie if she had found a job yet, and she said no, but that she would make a deal with the devil if she had to in order to keep her family alive and eating. "What do you mean?" I asked. "Would you deal [drugs] if you had to?" She looked away from me. "Yeah, I done it before, and I'll do it again. I mean I've never done it public or nothing, and I only did it during the holidays. I used to go to the club and get a table. I'd be there a couple of hours in the evening—only on weekends you know . . . Friday and Saturday." I asked her how much she would make. "I could pull in a 'G' [one thou-

sand dollars]. I never did it too much. But my kids should have stuff for the holidays. If I have to do that now, I guess I'll do whatever I have to."

In attempting to create viable households for themselves as single women or as mothers with children, the women in this ethnography engaged in a variety of strategies to reduce the probability of scarcity. These strategies for survival emerge within the context of violence and poverty and, as I hope is evident, are quite intentional.

The Black women whose experiences are told on the preceding pages of this book were caught in a trap of welfare engagement, where the consequence for the slightest infraction could be forced disengagement from government aid. As a result, the women identified ways to endure that were linked to the possibilities of accessing material resources (Bozzoli 1991). I think we may conceptualize these missions as strategies, even though they obviously do not reflect any sort of collective mobilization intended to address inequality. Yet we cannot presume that the sphere of collective action for social change is always accessible. Rather, we can carefully examine individual actions in which women engage to transform their lives and then determine the nodes of commonality around which they might organize, if they could. However, social justice is rarely satisfied with small incremental changes. But if we structure individual acts in terms of understanding the hierarchy of poor women's needs—that which makes a woman a little less poor, a little less regulated, a little more independent—then maybe success can be measured by a different standard.

In delineating the experiences of Black women who were battered and poor, I show they are neither pathetic, depraved, powerless victims, nor celebrated success stories of the antipoverty, battered women or antiwelfare reform movements. They are women who make decisions that were sometimes degrading because they had to. Therefore, their strategic missions should not be taken solely as a celebratory moment contextualized in a romantic assumption that welfare reform is working. Surviving against the odds should not be the human task. Negotiating constructed scarcity is not noble. It is a response to the structural violence that exists when institutions expose people to hazards that can impede one's well-being (Anglin 1998), such as sanctions and reduced benefits. Their strategic missions should be taken as a starting point to understand the sense that women make of their worlds resulting from constraints, by building kinship networks, by using speech acts, by developing instrumental friendships, and by engaging in illegal behaviors. I have resisted the tendency to create a typology of strategies that correspond to specific forms of violence, such as intimate violence, racism, and the structural violence of poverty. The point is to show that at the intersection of the forces of racism, intimate and structural violence, women try to develop webs of security. Appropriate or not, legal or not, their strategies represent a sort of architecture of safety in the absence of support by the state. By this I mean that women develop mechanisms to ensure their own survival against poverty policies that make it harder to live. Women figured out how to survive with jobs that paid too little and tenuous government entitlements. The strategies are generated within and in relation to the contexts of racism, sexism, poverty, and violence. These constructs do not permit for a neat chart depicting strategy on one axis and type of oppression on the other. It was hard to pinpoint if one strategy was unique to one set of issues, because the women are embodied with circumstances; they are all at once poor, Black, battered women, and their strategies are the "stuff" of everyday living, the practice of making it, when policy won't help.

9

Meticulous Rituals of Power
and Structural Violence

Historically welfare programs were implemented with the intent of protecting citizens against the fluctuations of life in an industrial society. Yet history has shown that welfare has not fully lived up to this intent. Policies and programs within welfare have regulated various aspects of social life, particularly in the area of labor—productive, domestic, and reproductive. And, as I have argued, the regulatory capability of welfare policy has had specific outcomes for women, outcomes that are differentiated by race. My goal has been to expose the ramifications of welfare reform for Black battered women and show the ways in which policy undermines their autonomy. It has also been my intention to examine the microsteps of welfare policy that disentitles and punishes women for not being in heterosexual relationships and offers a view of welfare reform policy as a form of extreme gender control linked to economic restructuring—that is a shift to a service economy and the perilous combination of gentrification and racialized residential patterns. Welfare reform-related activities, such as moving women into low-wage labor, forced child care arrangements, and housing restrictions, really illustrate how mechanisms of control are implemented in the most ordinary ways. As Sherita put it, welfare now was like "being on the inside," a reference associated with incarceration, where being monitored, scheduled, and detailed is the norm. To underscore the regulatory function of welfare policy, these case studies illustrate its particularly egregious impact on Black women. In this ethnography, I focused on one reason (of many) why some Black women use welfare—it is an outcome of the violence in their lives. The point has been to build on the emerging literature that connects two social problems—poverty and violence. The association between these social problems has led to an analysis showing that women are challenged by both violence and by the lack of access to resources. However, although challenged, women still attempted to formulate something that looks like "self-sufficiency," not because of welfare reform, but, rather, in spite of it.

I maintain that poor, Black, battered women, indeed, all women who are poor or lack access to material resources and choose, or need, welfare to gain independence, become caught in a "Kafkaesque-like web" (Mama 1989) of institutional relations. The U.S. policy toward the poor is designed to discipline and punish welfare recipients, proceeding from austere presumptions about poor people. To explain the punitive measures and outcomes, I use the term "institutional entanglement," which describes the phenomenon of poor women being controlled through welfare reform. It expresses the sum total of the institutional experiences of poor women seeking to have their basic needs met. Institutional entanglement consists of monitoring women's performance and assessing their deficits and deviations. Judgments are passed, and the compulsion to control has ramifications beyond moving women off of welfare. Institutions (such as the Department of Social Services) dominate women's lives partially because they are cloaked behind the façade of authority and expertise, which masquerade as a kind of impartiality (Best and Kellner 1991: 57). It is this domination that I have tried to expose because:

> . . . the real political task in a society such as ours is to criticize the working of institutions which appear both neutral and independent; to criticize them in such a manner that the political violence which has always exercised itself obscurely through them will be

unmasked so that one can fight them. (Foucault 1974: 171)

Other anthropologists have interrogated the relations between institutions and individuals. Explaining how homeless people are bound to social service institutions, for example, Susser (1993) concludes that families with male children are organized through institutional mandates, which forbid male children over a certain age from living in some shelters with their mothers. Similarly, Liebow (1993) analyzes women living in homeless shelters and illustrates the ways in which the shelter system disciplines women by micromanaging their everyday lives, such as determining when they can sleep.

Foucault argues that regulatory practices are utilized to create the "docile bodies that are needed in a rational and efficient society" (Merquior 1985: 94). I suggest welfare reform policy as translated by the River Valley County Department of Social Services attempts to transform Black battered women on welfare into docile bodies to divert them from the rolls (chapter 4); to serve the labor needs of the county (chapter 5); to reconfigure mothering (chapter 6), and to contain them in specific residential areas (chapter 7).

The practices to achieve docility are aptly defined by Staples (1997), who argues that the microtechniques of social control are "meticulous rituals of power." They include knowledge-gathering activities—small procedures that are faithfully repeated and are intended to discipline people into acting in certain ways (Staples 1997: 3). While Staples points out that these rituals of power exist in the dominant/subordinate relationships between managers and workers; parents and children; teachers and students; they also take place on a larger scale between individuals and public institutions.

Meticulous rituals of power in which institutional engagement is exacted involve documenting social life elicited through face-to-face interviews with social service personnel and developing a network of mandates that regulates poor women's behavior in terms of their work, where they live, and how they parent. In the end, however, the meticulous rituals of power both cause and exacerbate scarcity and reinforce hierarchical arrangements of inequality.

We may conclude that welfare reform policy represents a complex regime of control that differentiates labor and reinforces gender and race relations and legitimizes inequality. Inequalities are imposed when people are not given a chance to go to school or pursue jobs of their choice, and when, as Anglin (1998) notes, "government policies valorize particular family forms (the nuclear family) and punish other forms of family (single women with children) through programs that resolve local and national budgetary problems by withdrawing social support from the undeserving" (145). The Black women in this ethnography are examples of subjects disciplined through policy at the intersection of violence, race, and poverty.

The Structural Violence of Policy

Intense levels of bureaucracy govern and order women, and they are also controlled by the economy of the county in which they lived. The interaction of these factors hindered achieving "self-sufficiency" and engendered a set of strategies by some women, as they attempted to amend their experiences. While I argue that welfare reform policy mimics historical forms of regulation, it also authors new scripts of control within the context of the global economy. I, therefore, also suggest that welfare reform is structural violence. We may view the complexity of violence, race, poverty, and local responses to global shifts converging in policies that produce forms of domination and that subvert people's chances for survival (Anglin 1998).

A symbol of the structural violence of the policy can be found in the mirror that recipients are supposed to look into in the training room at the Department of Labor, referred to in *No Magic In the Market*. That mirror asks them to look at themselves as America wants to see them, which paradoxically demands their invisibility. Looking in the mirror also demands a form of self-governance that both situates and generates individual blame for being unemployable, unable to find neither housing, and unable to locate child care. Governmentality of this sort has been viewed by Cruikshank (1993), as a shift in terrains of responsibility toward the self, self-policing, self-care, and away from social commitment (Lyon-Callo 2004). Further, there's a psychic violence here constructed by the pretense that nothing matters—not even race—as long as one participates in the magic of the market. And, although work may be viewed as crucial for human development (Raphael 2000), as it is constructed within the global economy, and the locally distressed and simultaneously resurgent economy in River Valley, there is little or no opportunity for much beyond basic survival.

Therefore, I suggest that welfare reform may be viewed as another form of violence, in this case structural violence, because women are unable to earn a living wage. Most welfare-to-work jobs pay minimum wage at most. Almost all are in the service sector, which means they are rarely full-time and almost never include benefits. The term structural violence, originally used by Johan Galtung (1969), refers to any constraint on human potential due to economic and political circumstances that structure or exacerbate inequality. Structural violences may seem ordinary and are often invisible because they are normalized by being institutionalized. Used here the term helps to explain welfare reform's impact by teasing out the multiple constraints battered Black women face due to the synergistic effects of global restructuring and neoliberal social policies, both of which emphasize such measures as privatization and the provision of social programs via competitive so-called free markets. As such, women experience violence beyond the physical. So, while physical violence may create and sustain poverty, the structural violence of policy mandates sustains inequalities and inaccessibility to critical resources, leaving poverty unresolved.

Clearly the details of how effective welfare reform has been in subjugating women can be connected to the economy of River Valley County and the proliferation of service industries. The county's overdependence on one corporation placed it in a precarious position, nearly devastating, the upstate region. The consequences were typical of those across the United States, where corporate contraction and downsizing have burdened a number of localities. What ensued were high rates of unemployment, abandonment of buildings, and a depleted economic base. These conditions changed Laneville into more of an "urban ghetto" with the attendant social ills.

However, these were the same conditions that also made the city ripe for revitalization, and became a domain for reinvestment and the restructuring of social and economic and geographic space. Out of these circumstances, welfare reform was easy to implement, as poor women are bonded to departments of social services, assuming key roles in economic development as the labor force of choice for a growing service sector.

The logic of forced participation in the low-wage service sector is also a logic of exclusion from social and economic mobility, as stratification is institutionalized against those who constitute the "fringes." Ultimately this logic interferes with the human capacity to flourish. In other words, the quality of life is forsaken. The restrictive, exclusionary elements of welfare reform are counterintuitive to the stated priority of fostering "self-sufficiency" among recipients who require government assistance.

"Self-Sufficiency"

Institutional entanglement compromises "self-sufficiency," and regulatory rituals hinder basic liberties. Kittay (1999) identifies these basic liberties as freedom of movement, choice of occupation, income, and wealth and the social bases for self-respect. All of these liberties are restrained under welfare reform. Freedom of choice is virtually nonexistent; women are unable to work in occupations in which they are interested because the mandate to work may not include their choice of occupation. Women are not always able to live in areas in which they feel safe or find desirable because the income maintenance provided by Social Services restricts their options. Women cannot choose to stay home with their newborns or young children. Then, as a result of sanctions, women's lives become even more restricted, as they are forced to patch together ways to eat, pay rent, and obtain child care.

In paying attention to Black women, we can see how power and control are exerted in relation to race. By paying attention to battered women, we are forced to consider how control operates even under circumstances that might mitigate against its necessity. That is to say, one might assume that a level of institutional sympathy would accompany a victim of violence, but as this ethnography shows, this is not the case; institutions are not organized by sympathy. Instead, what we find in detailing Black, battered women's experiences is how welfare reform exerts power toward the fringes, at the extremity of society at the level of ongoing subjugation, and in the process undermines the project of "self-sufficiency."

While it is assumed that entry into the labor market will lead to independence and "self-sufficiency," here we see that the dynamic of violence, race, and policy run interference. The notion of "self-sufficiency" as an answer to poverty is flawed because it does not emerge in the contexts, which have been described here. Pushing people to participate in "democratic capitalism" by moving them from welfare into low-paying, insecure jobs must be reconsidered, given that welfare reform policy "expropriates vital economic and non-material resources, subverting chances for survival" (Anglin, 1998).

Connolly (2000) astutely notes that the language of "self-sufficiency" and independence is a false vocabulary. Independence, as defined by the welfare state, is fictive. Kittay (1999) argues that the welfare state resists acknowledgment of its obligation to the social order. Welfare policy's rendition of independence is based on inadequate knowledge of the contexts and circumstances of people's lives and does not assume that race and class status or longer-term needs will leak their way into women's lives or into the evaluations of the social service caseworkers, landlords, or employers. More important, welfare reform policy and its focus on work is not concerned about the quality of life that women in need desire or deserve. Without factoring these points into the equation, we find policy that places women at risk and attempts to limit their chances to decide what is in their own best interests. But they still act as agents of their lives while trying to move beyond being caught between a rock and a hard place.

Notes

Chapter 1

1. Nonlethal forms of intimate violence include rape, assault, and aggravated assault.

2. The women in the study are demographically similar to the national welfare caseload. Generally about 90% of TANF recipients are women. In 2000 the average age of a welfare recipient was 31 years old and half had a formal education of 12 years or more. In terms of race, in 2000, 31% of the welfare caseload was White, 39% were Black, and and 22% were Hispanic. All data is from the Department of Health and Human Services.

Chapter 2

1. It is not that people in the United States had not been poor prior to 1935. Rather the Social Security Act marked the first federal, as opposed to local, response in addressing relief (Piven and Cloward 1993). The type of federal programs that existed prior to the Social Security Act of 1935 created jobs, such as the Federal Emergency Relief Administration (FERA); Works Projects Administration (WPA), Public Works Administration (PWA), which provided construction jobs; and the Civilian Conservation Corps, which organized work in forestry and conservation (see Patterson 1994).

2. Financial aid to the mother or caretaker of the children was added in 1950.

3. For a detailed analysis of the role of the Civil Rights Movement in making the welfare state more responsive to Blacks, see Quadagno 1994.

4. This is the term I use to describe the constructed identity of Black women on welfare, by political, academic and media elites, which is laden with ideas of Black women's sexuality.

5. In its annual report on the State of Black America, The National Urban League found that one of the most alarming issues in relation to Blacks was job market statistics. The results show that Blacks are losing their jobs twice as fast as Whites. According to the Bureau of Labor Statistics, the national average for June 2002 was 5.9%. When broken down, the national average for Whites was 5.2, and for Blacks it was 10.7.

6. New Jersey was the first state to institute the family cap in 1992, whereby incremental benefits were eliminated for the birth of additional children. The law provided no exceptions, including births that result from rape, incest, failed contraception, or multiple births to the family cap. For example, with the birth of a fourth child, a family of three receiving AFDC was forced to survive on a benefit level calculated for a family of three.

Chapter 3

1. The antiviolence movement was crucial in the passage of the Violence Against Women Act (VAWA) in 1994. VAWA allocated $1,620,000,000 in funding, for all states from 1995 to 2000. Grants were used to remedy the systemic barriers that survivors of violence face. The barriers included offering education and training for judges in state and federal courts, conducting research, and increasing funding to battered women's shelters.

2. New York City began funding domestic violence shelters in 1978. At that time, New York was in the midst of a fiscal crisis and on the brink of bankruptcy. With no funding available to build housing for battered women, it was decided that domestic violence shelters should be paid for in the same way as homeless shelters: by using funds that people receive from social service. A reimbursement scheme was developed to direct money, which would ordinarily be made as payment to the client or as direct payment to a landlord, to the shelter based on a per diem rate.

Chapter 4

1. Because Gloria is a single adult, she is eligible to receive Safety Net Assistance formerly known as Home Relief. She had a prior case with Social Services, which was indicated in her case record file at RVCDSS. All case record files include, but are not limited to: the recipient's application, birth certificate, pay stubs, and notes taken by the caseworker during each interview (New York State Department of Social Services 1995b).

2. Unlike any of the other women interviewed, Leslie decided she wanted to write her life history for me, not have it tape recorded.

3. "If you are pregnant and under 18 or are a parent who is under 18 and not married, you must live with a parent, legal guardian, or other relative. If your worker determines that this is not possible or not in your child's best interest, the local DSS will decide if your current living arrangement is appropriate. If it is not, the local DSS will assist you in finding other appropriate living arrangements" (New York State Department of Social Services 1997a: 5).

4. In the United States teenage childbearing is much higher than in other industrialized nations. For example, in the early 1990s the rate of teenage births was two times higher in the United States than in Great Britain, four times higher than in Sweden or Spain, and 15 times higher than in Japan. It is not that teens in the United States are more sexually active, but rather that they use birth control less frequently and less effectively.

5. Implementation of the Family Violence Option in New York was comprehensive, including the mandate that local New York districts offer universal notification of the violence option to all public assistance applicants. To facilitate caseworkers' ability to screen for domestic violence and understand the role of the Option, the New York State Office of Children and Family Services and the Office for the Prevention of Domestic Violence produced the video "Domestic Violence and the Family Violence Option."

6. States may waive recipients from requirements for almost any length of time that they choose. Some have no time limits on temporary exemptions, while others permit exemptions for 90 days, 12 months, or 24 months. In addition some states allow for renewal of waivers.

7. A Welfare Reform Committee in River Valley County had organized a number of organizations and people to serve as

monitors, to document human rights violations. The violations were linked to changes in welfare laws, regulations, and their implementation by the River Valley County Department of Social Services.

Chapter 5

1. The occupations with the highest net annual openings between 1998 and 2008 were food preparation workers, waiters and waitresses; janitors and cleaners; home health aides; and correction officers and jailers. (Occupational Outlook 1998–2008 and Wages).

2. According to the State Metropolitan Area Data Book (www.census.gov/staab/ww/smadb.htm) there were more than 18,000 people employed in retail establishments, and over 30,000 people were employed in the service sector in River Valley County.

3. The Private Industry Council is an administrative outgrowth of the Job Training Partnership Act (JTPA), which was a bipartisan bill presented by Senators Ted Kennedy (Democrat) and Dan Quayle (Republican) signed in 1986. At the time the legislation was signed, the intent of JTPA was to serve the needs of people who were eligible under Title I and Title II funding of the Act. Title I eligible people include dislocated workers—people laid off from their jobs and unemployed for 15 weeks, displaced homemakers, and people over the age of 55. Under Welfare-to-Work, PIC also has a training program where services are provided after a person is attached to work. The training is for people who have not been employed or are not considered displaced. The funding for their training comes under Title II. The qualifications to participate in the program are: 1) A person must be receiving Temporary Assistance to Needy Families, 2) The person must have been on social services for 30 months and currently receiving services, and 3) They must have a fairly low skill level in math and reading. To be eligible to participate in the PIC program, a participant must have a score of 8.9 or below. Once a person has been assessed and certified as eligible to participate, they receive training. If they require skills building, then PIC provides that service. If a person needs what is called "up-the-ladder" training, (such as a certificate, so they can get a promotion) then PIC will provide that as well. The target population for PIC's welfare-to-work program is so stringent that only 12 people had enrolled as of April 2000.

4. Service occupations include: private household work, such as child care, cleaners, and servants; protective services, such as police

officers, guards, and firefighters; food preparation workers including cooks, waiters/waitresses/counter, and kitchen workers; health service workers including dental assistants, health aides, nursing aides; cleaning staff, maids, janitors, and barbers, hairdressers, family care providers and teachers assistants.

5. The Job Club was strictly for AFDC recipients because it was a demonstration project that grew out of the federally funded food stamp program in the 1980s. Federal funds could not be used for Home Relief (single people) recipients. However, River Valley County found the program to be so successful, they chose to use County dollars to fund the program.

6. An employable demeanor is achieved by assessing and certifying recipients over a 3-day period. One's educational level is determined as well as one's vocational capacity. Trainees are then offered workshops on how to prepare for a job. It was pointed out to me by one advocate, Adolphus, that it is probably best that assessments are done by external agencies such as PIC and BOCES because:

> *To have Social Service employees conduct assessments may be disastrous for some people who have had long-term relationships with RVCDSS staff. If those interactions had in any way been negative, then RVCDSS staff might make assessments based on retaliation, which would hinder clients' ability to secure appropriate training.*

Chapter 6

1. The first ADC program was enacted at the prerogative of the Illinois Fund to Parents Act in 1911, following an endorsement of the idea, in 1909, that if mothers were fit and proper their families should be supported (see Leff 1983).

Chapter 7

1. This allocation was the amount Leslie received until the baby's birth. After the birth, the increase in the number of people in the household would raise her housing allowance up to $469.

2. Housing experts suggest that a 5% vacancy rate is indicative of a healthy rental market. But the rate in River Valley County is

2%. Subsidized housing complexes have waiting lists, which suggests a negative vacancy rate. Of the nearly 20 subsidized buildings in the City of Laneville, only 3 did not have waiting lists, and 1 of the 3 is for senior citizens. A negative vacancy rate means that women will have difficulty moving into even low-income housing units.

3. Just 5 months before signing the Personal Responsibility and Work Opportunity Reconciliation Act, President Clinton signed the Housing Opportunity Program Extension Act. This was another piece of legislation aimed at shredding poor people's supports. For a discussion of how this policy impacts battered women, see Renzetti 2001.

4. The difference between a voucher and a certificate is that with a Section 8 Certificate the maximum allowable rent is based on room size and adjusted gross income for a particular area. On an annual basis Housing and Urban Development (HUD) publishes the fair market rents for each area. The rent cannot exceed the established amount. In River Valley County, the Fair Market Rent (FMR) for a one bedroom is $732. Alternatively, a Section 8 Voucher allows people to make above the income limits and move into nontarget areas, where rents might be a little more expensive. Rental payments are standardized at 90 to 110% of the FMR set by HUD. These percentages apply because rents in the City of Laneville are cheaper than in other parts of the county. With a voucher a person can move into an apartment with rent that is above the limit, if they pay 30% of the difference between the payment standard and the actual cost of the rent. With a certificate you must stay within the fair market rate. As of October 2000, the Section 8 program was based on the voucher system.

Bibliography

Abramovitz, Mimi. *Regulating the Lives of Women: Social Welfare Policy from Colonial Times to the Present.* Boston, MA: South End Press, 1996.

Alan Guttmacher Institute. *Teenage Pregnancy: Overall Trends and State-by-State Information.* New York: Alan Guttmacher Institute, 1999.

Ammons, Linda. "Mules, Madonnas, Babies, Bathwater, Racial Imagery and Stereotypes: The African-American Woman and the Battered Woman Syndrome." *Wisconsin Law Review,* 1995.

Amott, Teresa L. "Black women and AFDC." *Women, the State and Welfare.* Ed. Linda Gordon. Madison: University of Wisconsin Press, 1990: 280–298.

Amott, Teresa, and Julie A. Matthaei. *Race, Gender and Work: A Multicultural Economic History of Women in the United States.* Boston, MA: South End Press, 1991.

Angel House. 2000. *1999 Shelter Statistics.*

Angel House Newsletter. 1996.

Anglin, Mary. "Feminist Perspectives on Structural Violence." *Identities* 5.2 (1998): 145–151.

Auletta, Ken. *The Underclass.* New York: Random House, 1982.

Barbee, Evelyn. "Ethnicity and Woman Abuse in the United States." *Violence Against Women: Nursing Research, Education and Practice Issues.* Ed. Carolyn M. Sampselle. New York: Hemisphere Publishing Corporation, n.d., 153–166.

Bassuk, Ellen L., Linda F. Weinreb, John C. Buckner, Angela Brown, Amay Salomon, and Shari S. Bassuk. "The Characteristics and Needs of Sheltered Homeless and Low-Income Housed Mothers." *Journal of the American Medical Association* 276.8 (1996): 640–646.

Bell, Winifred. *Aid to Families With Dependent Children.* New York: Columbia University Press, 1965.

Behar, Ruth and Deborah A. Gordon. *Women Writing Culture.* Berkeley: University of California Press, 1995.

Best, Steven, and Douglas Kellner. *Postmodern Theory: Critical Interrogations.* New York: The Guilford Press, 1991.

Boo, Katherine. "The Churn: Creative Destruction in a Border Town." *The New Yorker,* 29 March 2004.

Bozzoli, Belinda. *Women of Phokeng: Consciousness, Life Strategy, and Migrancy in South Africa, 1900–1983.* Portsmouth, NH: Heinemann Educational Books, Inc., 1991.

Brandwein, Ruth, ed. *Battered Women, Children and Welfare Reform: The Ties that Bind.* Thousand Oaks, CA: Sage Publications, 1999.

Brewer, Rose. "Black Women in Poverty: Some Comments on Female-Headed Families." *Signs* 13.2 (1988): 331–339.

Cantave, Cassandra, and Roderick Harrison. Joint Center for Political and Economic Studies. June 1999. *http://www. jointcenter.org/DB/printer/employ.htm.*

Caviness, Yvonne Gault. "The Mommy Club: Black Stay-at-Home Mothers Look to One Another for Support." *Essence Magazine,* August 2002.

Center for Law and Social Policy, CLASP Update: A CLASP Report on Welfare Reform. *Domestic Violence Victims Face More Barriers: Wisconsin.* Washington, D.C.: Center for Law and Social Policy, 2000.

Child Trends. *New Research, Latest State-level Data Available on Teen Sexual Behavior, Pregnancy and Births.* Washington, D.C., 1997. Cited in Jody Raphael. *Saving Bernice: Battered Women, Welfare and Poverty.* Boston, MA: Northeastern University Press, 2000.

Collins, Patricia Hill. *Black Feminist Thought: Knowledge, Consciousness, and the Politics of Empowerment.* New York: Routledge, 1990.

Collins, Randall. *Sociology of Marriage and the Family: Gender, Love, and Property.* Chicago: Nelson-Hall, 1988.

Connolly, Deborah R. *Homeless Mothers: Face to Face With Women and Poverty.* Minneapolis and London: University of Minnesota Press, 2000.

Crittenden, Anne. *The Price of Motherhood: Why the Most Important Job in the World Is Still the Least Valued.* New York: Owl Books, 2002.

Cruikshank, Barbara. "Revolutions Within: Self-Government and Self-Esteem." *Economy and Society* 22.3 (1993): 327–44.

Curcio, William. "The Passaic County Study of AFDC Recipients in a Welfare-to-Work Program: A Preliminary Analysis." Paterson, NJ: Passaic County Board of Social Services, 1997.

Davis, Dána-Ain. "Manufacturing Mammies: The Burdens of Service Work and Welfare Reform Among Battered Black Women." *Anthropologica.* 46.2 (2004): 273–288.

———. Narrating The Mute: Race, Racializing and Racism in a Neo-liberal Economy. Paper presented at the Society for the Anthropology of North America Annual Conference, Merida, Mexico. 3–8 May 2005.

———. "What Did You Do Today? Notes From a Politically Engaged Anthropologist." *Urban Anthropology.* 32.2 (2003): 147–174.

Davis, Martha. "The Economics of Abuse: How Violence Perpetuates Poverty." *Battered Women, Children and Welfare Reform: The Ties That Bind.* Ed. Ruth Brandwein. Thousand Oaks, CA: Sage Publications, 1999. 17–30.

Davis, Martha F., and Susan J. Kraham. "Protecting Women's Welfare in the Face of Violence." *Fordham Urban Law Journal* 22.4 (1995): 11–41.

Dehavenon, Anna Lou, and Anne Okongwu. "Policy Planning for Single Female-Headed Households: What Is Needed in the United States." *Where Did All The Men Go? Female-Headed/Female-Supported Households in Cross-Cultural Perspective.* Ed. Joan P. Mencher and Anne Okongwu. Boulder, CO: Westview Press, 1993. 253–272.

Desjarlais, Robert. *Shelter Blues: Sanity and Selfhood Among the Homeless.* Philadelphia, PA: University of Pennsylvania Press, 1997.

Dobash, R. Emerson, and Russell P. Dobash. *Women, Violence and Social Change.* London: Routledge, 1992.

Dollard, John. *Caste and Class in a Southern Town.* Madison: University of Wisconsin Press, 1937.

Domke, David, Kelley McCoy, and Marcos Torres. "News Media, Racial Perceptions, and Political Cognition." *Communication Research* 26.5 (1999): 570–607.

Drew, Paul, and John Heritage, eds. *Talk at Work: Interaction in Institutional Settings.* Cambridge: Cambridge University Press, 1992.

Edin, Kathryn, and Laura Lein. *Making Ends Meet: How Single Mothers Survive Welfare and Low Wage Work.* New York: Russell Sage Foundation, 1997.

Fitchen, Janet M. *Poverty in Rural America: A Case Study.* Prospect Heights, IL: Waveland Press, 1981.

Flanagan, Caitlin. "How Serfdom Saved the Women's Movement." *The Atlantic Online.* March 2004. *www.theatlantic.com/issues/2004/03/flanagan.htm.*

Frazier, E. Franklin. *The Negro Family in the United States.* Chicago: University of Chicago Press, 1939.

Foucault, Michel. *The Order of Things.* New York: Vintage Books, 1974.

Gal, Susan. "Between Speech and Silence: The Problematics of Research on Language and Gender." *Gender at the Crossroads of Knowledge: Feminist Anthropology in the Postmodern Era.* Ed. Micaela di Leonardo. Berkeley: University of California Press, 1991: 175–203.

Galtung, Johan. "Violence, Peace, and Peace Research." *Journal of Peace Research* 6 (1969): 170–171.

Garfield, Gail. *Knowing What We Know: African-American Women's Experiences of Violence and Violations.* New Brunswick, NJ: Rutgers University Press, 2004.

Giannarelli, Linda, and James Barismantov. "Child-care Expenses of America's Families." *Assessing the New Federalism.* Washington, D.C.: The Urban Institute, 2000.

Gibbs, Nancy. "Making Time For a Baby." *Time.* 15 Apr. 2002.

Gilder, George. "Welfare's New Consensus." *Public Interest* 8 Fall (1987): 20–25.

———. *Wealth and Poverty*. New York: Basic Books, 1981.

Gilens, Martin. *Why Americans Hate Welfare*. Chicago: University of Chicago Press, 1999.

Gilligan, James. *Violence: Our Deadly Epidemic and Its Causes*. New York: Putnam, 1996.

Goode, Victor M., and Conrad A. Johnson. "Emotional Harm in Housing Discrimination Cases: A New Look at a Lingering Problem." *Fordham Urban Law Journal* (2003).

Gooden, Susan T. "All Things Not Being Equal: Differences in Case-worker Support Toward Black and White Welfare Clients." *Harvard Journal of African-American Public Policy* 4 (1998): 23–33.

———. "The Hidden Third Party: Welfare Recipients' Experiences with Employers." *Journal of Public Management and Social Policy* 5.1 (1999): 6–83.

Gordon, Linda. "Family Violence, Feminism and Social Control." *Women, The State and Welfare*. Ed. Linda Gordon. Madison: University of Wisconsin Press, 1990. 178–199.

———. *Pitied But Not Entitled*. New York: Free Press, 1994.

Gordon, Rebecca. *Cruel and Usual: How Welfare "Reform" Punishes Poor People*. Oakland, CA: Applied Research Center, 2001.

Greenfield, L. "Violence by Intimates: Analysis of Data on Crimes by Current or Former Spouses, Boyfriends and Girlfriends." Bureau of Justice Statistics Factbook, Washington, D.C.: United States Department of Justice, March 1998. NCJ–167237.

Green-Powell, Patricia. "Methodological Considerations in Field Research: Six Case Studies." *Oral Narrative Research with Black Women*. Ed. Kim Marie Vaz. Thousand Oaks, CA: Sage Publications, 1997. 197–222.

Gutman, Herbert. *The Black Family in Slavery and Freedom, 1750–1925*. New York: Pantheon Books, 1976.

Hancock, Ange-Marie. *The Politics of Disgust: The Public Identity of the Welfare Queen*. New York: New York University Press, 2004.

Handler, Joel F. *The Poverty of Welfare Reform*. New Haven, CT: Yale University Press, 1995.

Harley, Sharon, ed. *Sister Circle: Black Women and Work.* New Brunswick, NJ: Rutgers University Press, 2002.

Hearn, Marcellene E. *Dangerous Indifference: New York City's Failure to Implement the Family Violence Option.* New York: NOW Legal Defense and Education Fund for Women, 2000.

Henly, Julia R. *Challenges to Finding and Keeping Jobs in the Low-Skilled Labor Market.* Paper presented at the 20th Annual Meeting of the Association for Public Policy Analysis and Management, New York, 1998.

Hill, Robert B. *The Strengths of African American Families: Twenty-five Years Later.* University Press of America, 1999.

Hoff, Lee Ann. *Battered Women as Survivors.* New York: Routledge, 1990.

Holzer, Harry J. "Will Employers Hire Welfare Recipients? Recent Survey Evidence from Michigan." *Journal of Policy Analysis Management* 18.3 Summer (1999): 449–472.

Holzer, Harry J., and Michael A. Stoll. "Employer Demand for Welfare Recipients by Race." Joint Center for Poverty Research. Working Paper, 197 07–18–2000.

James, Joy. *Resisting State Violence: Radicalism, Gender and Race in U.S. Culture.* Minneapolis: University of Minnesota Press, 1996.

Jewell, K. Sue. *From Mammy to Miss America and Beyond: Cultural Images and The Shaping of U.S. Social Policy.* London and New York: Routledge, 1993.

Jones, Jacqueline. *The Dispossessed: America's Underclass From the Civil War to the Present.* New York: Basic Books, 1992.

Kalil, Ariel, Heidi Schweingruber, Marijata Daniel-Echols, and Ashli Breen. "Mother, Worker, Welfare Recipient: Welfare Reform and the Multiple Roles of Low-income Women." *Coping with Poverty: The Social Contexts of Neighborhood, Work, and Family in the African-American Community.* Ed. Sheldon Danziger and Ann Chih Lin. Ann Arbor: The University of Michigan Press, 2000: 201–223.

Kanuha, Valli. "Domestic Violence, Racism, and the Battered Women's Movement in the United States." *Future Interventions with Battered Women and Their Families.* Thousand Oaks, CA: Sage, 1996.

Kenney, Catherine T., and Karen R. Brown. *Report From the Front Lines: The Impact of Violence on Poor Women.* New York: NOW Legal Defense and Education Fund for Women. Women, Welfare and Abuse Working Group, 1996.

Kimmel, Jean. "The Role of Child Care Assistance." *Welfare Reform. Employment Research* 1.2 (1994): 1–3.

Kittay, Eva Feder. "Welfare, Dependency, and a Public Ethic of Care." *Whose Welfare?* Ed. Gwendolyn Mink. Ithaca, NY, and London: Cornell University Press, 1999. 189–213.

Kurz, Demie. "Women, Welfare and Domestic Violence." *Whose Welfare?* Ed. Gwendolyn Mink. Ithaca, NY: Cornell University Press, 1999. 132–151.

Labov, William. *Language in the Inner City.* Philadelphia: University of Pennsylvania Press, 1972.

Ladner, Joyce. *Tomorrow's Tomorrow: The Black Woman.* New York: Doubleday, 1971.

Leff, Mark. "Consensus For Reform: The Mothers Pension Movement in the Progressive Era." *Social Service Review* 47 (1983): 397–417.

Lewis, Oscar. "The Culture of Poverty." *Scientific American* 215.4 (1966): 19–25.

Leibschutz, Sarah F. "Welfare Reform in New York: A Mixed Laboratory for Change." *Managing Welfare in Five States: The Challenge of Devolution.* Ed. Sarah F. Liebschutz. New York: The Rockefeller Institute Press, 2000. 57–76.

Lewis, Deborah Shaw, and Charmaine Crouse Yoest. *Mother in the Middle: Searching for Peace in the Mommy Wars.* Grand Rapids, MI: Zondervan, 1996.

Liebow, Elliot. *Tally's Corner: A Study of Negro Streetcorner Men.* London: Routledge and Kegan Paul, 1967.

———. *Tell Them Who I Am: The Lives of Homeless Women.* New York: Penguin Books, 1993.

Lopez, Iris. "Sterilization among Puerto Rican Women in New York City: Public Policy and Social Constraints." *Cities of the United States: Studies in Urban Anthropology.* Ed. Leith Mullings. New York: Columbia University Press, 1987. 269–291.

Loseke, Donilen R. *The Battered Woman and Shelters: The Social Construction of Wife Abuse.* Albany: State University of New York Press, 1992.

Lubiano, Wahneema. "Black Ladies, Welfare Queens, and State Minstrels: Ideological Wars by Narrative Means." *Race-ing Justice, En-gendering Power: Essays on Anita Hill, Clarence Thomas and the Construction of Social Reality.* Ed. Toni Morrison. New York: Pantheon Books, 1992. 323–363.

Luker, Kristin. *Dubious Conceptions: The Politics of Teenage Pregnancy.* Cambridge, MA: Harvard University Press, 1991.

Lyon-Callo, Vincent. *Inequality, Poverty, and Neoliberal Governance. Activist Ethnography in the Homeless Sheltering Industry.* Ontario, Canada: Broadview Press, 2004.

Mama, Amina. *The Hidden Struggle: Statutory and Voluntary Sector Responses to Violence Against Black Women in the Home.* London: London Race and Housing Research Unit, 1989.

Martin, Del. *Battered Wives.* New York: Pocket Books. 1976.

Massey, Douglas S., and Nancy A. Denton. *American Apartheid: Segregation and the Making of the Underclass.* Cambridge: Harvard University Press, 1992.

McElhinny, Bonnie. "Ideologies of Public and Private Language in Sociolinguistics." *Gender and Discourse.* Ed. Ruth Wodak. London, Thousand Oaks, New Delhi: Sage Publications, 1997. 106–139.

Mead, Lawrence M. *Beyond Entitlement: The Social Obligations of Citizenship.* New York: Free Press, 1986a.

———. *Workfare vs. Welfare.* Hearing before the Subcommittee on Trade, Productivity, and Economic Growth of the Joint Economic Committee, U.S. Congress, 99th Congress, 2nd Session, April 23, 1986. Washington, D.C.: Government Printing Office, 1986b, 98. Cited in Rickie Solinger. "Dependency and Choice: The Two Faces of Eve." *Whose Welfare,?* Ed. Gwendolyn Mink. Ithaca and London: Cornell University Press, 1999. 7–35.

Mencher, Joan P. 1993. "Female-headed, Female-supported Households in India: Who Are They and What are Their Survival Strategies?" *Where Did All The Men Go?: Female-headed, Female-supported Households in Cross Cultural Perspective.* Ed. Joan P. Mencher and Ann Okongwu. Boulder, CO: Westview Press, 1993. 203–232.

Merquior, J. G. *Foucault*. Berkeley, CA: University of California Press, 1985.

Mink, Gwendolyn. "The Lady and the Tramp: Gender, Race, and the Origins of the American Welfare State." *Women, The State and Welfare*. Ed. Linda Gordon. Madison: University of Wisconsin Press, 1990. 92–124.

———. *Welfare's End*. Ithaca, NY: Cornell University Press, 1998.

———, ed. *Whose Welfare?* Ithaca, NY, and London, Cornell University Press, 1999.

Morgen, Sandra, and Jeff Maskovsky. "The Anthropology of Welfare 'Reform': New Perspectives on U.S. Urban Poverty in the Post-Welfare Era." *Annual Review of Anthropology*. 32(1) 2003: 315–338.

Moynihan, Daniel P. *The Negro Family: The Case for National Action*. Washington, D.C. U.S. Government Printing Office, 1965.

Mullings, Leith. "Anthropological Perspectives on the Afro-American Family." *American Journal of Social Psychiatry* 6 (Winter 1986): 1.

———. "Images, Ideology, and Women of Color." *Women of Color in U.S. Society*. Ed. Maxine Baca Zinn and Bonnie Thornton Dill. Philadelphia, PA: Temple University Press, 1994. 265–290.

Mullings, Leith and Alaka Wali. *Stress and Resilience: The Social Context of Reproduction in Central Harlem*. New York: Kluwer Academic/Plenum Publishers, 2001.

National Center for Policy Analysis. "Better Off Welfare." Dallas, TX: 2002. *http://www.ncpa.org/pub/st/st255/st255c.html* (Accessed May 21, 2005).

National Low Income Housing Coalition. *Out Of Reach*. Washington, D.C.: National Low Income Housing Coalition, 1999. *www.nlihc.org*.

National Urban League. "The State of Black America" 2004. *www.nul.org/pdf/sobaexec.pdf* (Accessed March 2004).

Nelson, Barbara J. "The Origins of the Two-channel Welfare State." *Women, The State and Welfare*. Ed. Linda Gordon. Madison: University of Wisconsin Press, 1990. 152–177.

Neubuck, Kenneth, and Nathan Cazenave. *Welfare Racism: Playing the Race Card Against America's Poor*. New York: Routledge, 2001.

Newman, Katherine. *No Shame in My Game: The Working Poor in the Inner City.* New York: Alfred A. Knopf and The Russell Sage Foundation, 1999.

New York State Department of Labor. "Economic Development Services Unit." May: P440. New York: New York State Department of Labor, 1998.

New York State Department of Social Services. "The Domestic Violence Prevention Act." 1995 Annual Report to the Governor and Legislature. New York: New York State Department of Social Services, 1995a.

———. "What You Should Know About Your Rights and Responsibilities." Book 1. DSS-4148A. New York: New York State Department of Social Services, 1995b.

———. "New Information about Public Assistance and Food Stamps." LDSS-4148D. New York: New York State Department of Social Services, 1997a.

New York State Office of Temporary Disability. *Temporary and Disability Assistance Statistics.* New York: New York State Office of Temporary Disability, 1999.

Okun, Lewis. *Woman Abuse: Facts Replacing Myths.* Albany: State University of New York Press, 1986.

Pardo, Italo. *Managing Existence in Naples: Morality, Action and Structure.* Cambridge: Cambridge University Press, 1996.

Patterson, James T. *America's Struggle Against Poverty 1900–1994.* Cambridge, MA: Harvard University Press, 1994.

Petchesky, Rosalind Pollack. "The Body as Property: A Feminist Revision." *Conceiving The New World Order: The Global Politics of Reproduction.* Ed. Faye D. Ginsburg and Rayna Rapp. Berkeley: University of California Press, 1995. 387–406.

Piven, Frances Fox. "Welfare and Work." *Whose Welfare?* Ed. Gwendolyn Mink. Ithaca, NY, and London: Cornell University Press, 1999. 83–99.

Piven, Frances Fox, and Richard Cloward. *Poor People's Movements.* New York: Vintage Books, 1979.

———. *Regulating the Poor: The Functions of Public Welfare.* New York: Vintage Books, 1993.

Polakow, Valerie. *Lives On The Edge: Single Mothers and Their Children in The Other America.* Chicago, IL: University of Chicago Press, 1993.

———. "Savage Distributions: Welfare Myths and Daily Lives." *A New Introduction to Poverty: The Role of Race, Power and Politics.* Ed. Louis Kushnick and James Jennings. New York: New York University Press, 1999a. 241–262

———. "The Shredded Net: The End of Welfare As We Knew It." *A New Introduction to Poverty: The Role of Race, Power and Politics.* Ed. Louis Kushnick and James Jennings. New York: New York University Press, 1999b. 167–184.

Powdermaker, Hortense. *After Freedom: A Cultural Study in the Deep South.* New York: Atheneum (1939), reissued 1967).

Prashad, Vijay. *Keeping Up with the Dow Joneses: Debt, Prison, Workfare.* Cambridge, MA: South End Press, 2003.

"President Clinton's Announcement on Welfare Legislation." *New York Times*, 1 August, 1996, National Desk.

Quadagno, Jill. *The Color of Welfare: How Racism Undermined the War on Poverty.* New York: Oxford University Press, 1994.

Quint, Janet, Kathryn Edin, Maria L. Buck, et. al. *Big Cities and Welfare Reform: Early Implementation and Ethnographic Findings From the Project on Devolution and Urban Change.* New York: Manpower Demonstration Research Corporation, 1999.

Ranney, David C. "Class, Race, Gender, and Poverty: A Critique of Some Contemporary Theories." *A New Introduction to Poverty: The Role of Race, Power and Politics.* Ed. Louis Kushnick and James Jennings. New York: New York University Press, 1999. 39–58.

Raphael, Jody. *Saving Bernice: Battered Women, Welfare and Poverty.* Boston: Northeastern University Press, 2000.

———. "The Family Violence Option: An Early Assessment." *Violence Against Women* 5.4 (1999): 449–466.

Raphael, Jody, and Tolman, Richard. *Trapped by Poverty, Trapped by Abuse: New Evidence Documenting the Relationship Between Domestic Violence and Welfare.* Illinois: Taylor Institute, 1997.

Rennison, Callie Marie, and Sarah Welchans. "Intimate partner violence." U.S. Department of Justice. *Bureau of Justice Statistics.* NCJ-178247. May 2000.

Renzetti, Claire. "One Strike and You're Out: Implications of a Federal Crime Control Policy for Battered Women." *Violence against Women* 7.6 (June 2001): 685–697.

Renzetti, Claire, and Shana L. Maier. "'Private' Crime in Public Housing: Fear of Crime and Violent Victimization among Women Public Housing Residents." Paper presented at the annual meeting of the Academy of Criminal Justice Sciences, Orlando, Florida, March 1999.

"Resident Civilian Labor Force Summary, New York State and Selected Areas." n.d.

Richie, Beth E. *Compelled to Crime: The Gender Entrapment of Battered Black Women.* New York: Routledge, 1996.

River Valley County Department of Social Services. *Temporary assistance/food stamp employment plan for January 1, 2000 to December 31, 2000.* New York: River Valley County Department of Social Services, 1999.

River Valley County Economic Development Corporation. *Annual Report.* New York, 1999.

Roberts, Dorothy. *Killing the Black Body: Race Reproduction and The Meaning of Liberty.* New York: Vintage Books, 1997.

———. "Welfare's Ban on Poor Motherhood." *Whose Welfare?* Ed. Gwendolyn Mink, Ithaca, NY, and London: Cornell University Press, 1999. 152–171.

Rodrique, Jessie M. "The Black Community and the Birth-control Movement." *Unequal Sisters: A Multi-cultural Reader in U.S. Women's History.* Ed. Ellen Carol DuBois and Vicki L. Ruiz. New York and London: Routledge, 1990. 333–354.

Ruben, Matthew. 2001. "Suburbanization and Urban Poverty under Neo-liberalism." *The New Poverty Studies: The Ethnography of Power, Politics, and Impoverished People in the United States.* Eds. Judith Goode and Jeff Maskovsky. New York: New York University Press, 2001. 435–469.

Salzinger, Leslie. "A Maid By Any Other Name." *Situated Lives: Gender and Culture in Everyday Life.* Eds. Louise Lamphere, Helena Ragone, and Patricia Zavella. New York, London: Routledge, 1997. 271–291.

Sassen-Koob, Saskia. "Labor Migrations and the New International Division of Labor." Eds. June Nash and M. Patricia Fernandez-Kelly. *Women, Men and the International Division of Labor.* Albany: State University of New York Press, 1983. 175–204.

Sassen, Saskia. "Analytic Borderlands: Race, Gender and Representations in the New City." *Re-presenting The City: Ethnicity, Capital and Culture in The 21st Century Metropolis.* Ed. Anthony D. King. New York: New York University Press, 1996. 183–202.

Schechter, Susan. *Women and Male Violence: The Visions and Struggles of the Battered Women's Movement.* Boston: South End Press, 1982.

Seccombe, Karen. *"So You Think I Drive a Cadillac?" Welfare Recipients' Perspectives on the System and Its Reform.* Boston, MA: Allyn and Bacon, 1999.

Shostak, Marjorie. "What The Wind Won't Take Away: The Genesis of Nisa—The Life and Words of a !Kung Woman." *Interpreting Women's Lives: Feminist Theory and Personal Narratives.* Ed. The Personal Narratives Group. Bloomington and Indianapolis: Indiana University Press, 1989. 228–240.

Skocpol, Theda. "The Limits of the New Deal System and the Roots of Contemporary Welfare Dilemmas." *The Politics of Social Policy in the United States.* Ed. Margaret Weir, Ann Shola Orloff, and Theda Skocpol. Princeton, N.J.: Princeton University Press, 1988.

———. *Protecting Soldiers and Mothers.* Cambridge, MA: Belknap. 1992.

Smith. Neil. *The New Urban Frontier: Gentrification and the Revanchist City.* London and NewYork: Routledge, 1996.

Solinger, Rickie. "Dependency and Choice: The Two Faces of Eve." *Whose Welfare?* Ed. Gwendolyn Mink. Ithaca, NY, and London: Cornell University Press, 1999. 7–35.

Stacey, Judith. "Can There Be a Feminist Ethnography?" *Women's Studies International Forum 11(1988):* 21–27.

Stack, Carol. *All Our Kin: Strategies for Survival in a Black Community.* New York: Harper and Row Publishers, 1974.

Staples, William G. *The Culture of Surveillance: Discipline and Social Control in the United States.* New York: St. Martin's Press, 1997.

Susser, Ida. "Creating Family Forms: The Exclusion of Men and Teenage Boys from Families in the New York City Shelter System, 1987–92." *Critique of Anthropology* 13.3 (1993): 267–284.

Tjaden, Patricia, and Nancy Thoennes. "Prevalence, Incidence and Consequences of Violence Against Women: Findings from the National Violence Against Women Survey." *Research in Brief*. Washington, D.C.: National Institute of Justice, U.S. Department of Justice, 1998.

Thomas, Susan L. "Race, Gender, and Welfare Reform: The Antinatalist Response." *Journal of Black Studies* 22.4 (1998): 419–446.

Turner, Margery Austin, Stephen L. Ross, George Galster, John Yinger. "Discrimination in Metropolitan Housing Markets: National Results from Phase I of HDS 2000." 2002.

United States Census Bureau. *Poverty 1999: People and Families in Poverty by Selected Characteristics: 1998 and 1999.* 2000. *www.census.gov/hhes/poverty/poverty99/pv99est1.html.*

———. Americas Families and Living Arrangements: 2003. P20–553. Washington, D.C., 2004.

United States Department of Commerce. *Mothers Who Receive AFDC Payments: Fertility and Socioeconomic Characteristics.* Washington D.C.: United States Department of Commerce, Economics and Statistics Administration, 1995.

United States Department of Justice. "Violence by Intimates: Analysis of Data on Crimes by Current or Former Spouses, Boyfriends, and Girlfriends." *Bureau of Justice Statistics*. NCJ-167237. Washington, D.C.: March 1998.

United States Department of Labor. "Facts on Working Women: Black Women in the Labor Force." Washington, D.C.: United States Department of Labor, 1997. *www.dol.gov/dol/wb/public/wb_pubs/bw1f97.htm.*

Wallis, Claudia. "The Case for Staying Home." *Time*. 22 March 2004.

Walters, Ronald. "The Democratic Party and Politics of Welfare Reform." *Social Policy and The Conservative Agenda*. Ed. Clarence Y. H. Lo and Michael Schwartz. Malden, MA: Blackwell Publishers Ltd, 1999. 37–52.

Websdale, Neil. *Policing the Poor: From Slave Plantation to Public Housing.* Boston: Northeastern University Press, 2001.

———. *Rural Woman Battering and the Justice System: An Ethnography.* Thousand Oaks, CA: Sage, 1998.

West, Guida. *The National Welfare Rights Movement: The Social Protest of Poor Women.* New York: Praeger Publishers, 1981.

Wilson, William Julius. "The Black Underclass." *The City Reader.* Ed. Richard T. LeGates and Frederic Stout. London: Routledge, 1984. 225–231.

Wolf, Eric. "Kinship, Friendship, and Patron-client Relations in Complex Societies." *The Social Anthropology of Complex Societies.* Ed. Michael Banton. London: Tavistock Publications, 1966.

Zucchino, David. *Myth of the Welfare Queen.* New York: Touchstone Books, 1999.

Zylan, Yvonne. "Maternalism Redefined: Gender, the State, and the Politics of Day Care, 1945–1962." *Gender & Society* 14.5 (2000): 608–629.

Index